To Kim,

With my warmest wishes,

[signature]

Hooked Rugs

HOOKED RUGS

History and the Continuing Tradition

Jessie A. Turbayne

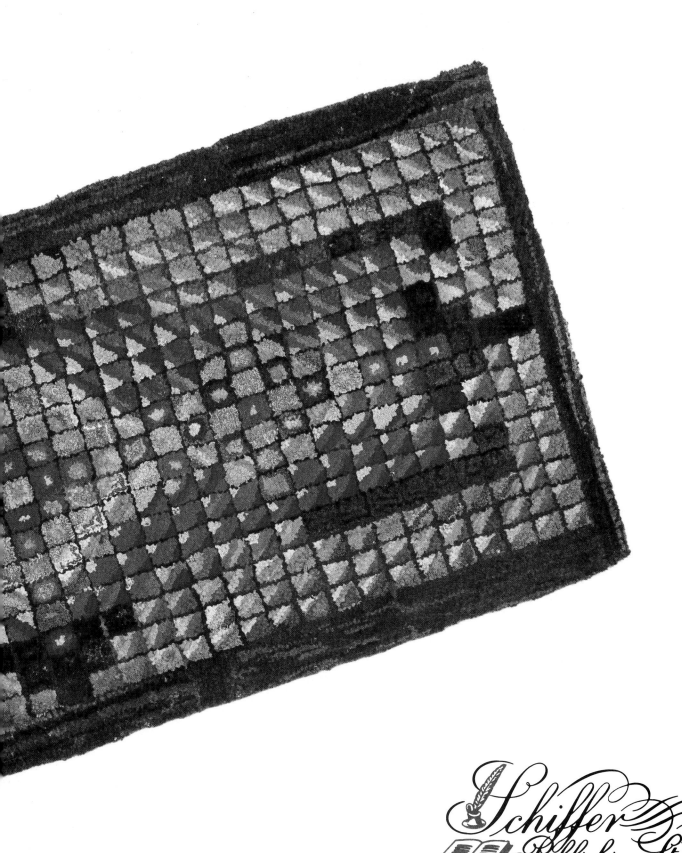

1469 Morstein Road, West Chester, Pennsylvania 19380

Dedication

For my mother and father, Jamie and Michael

A horse's head adorned with a bridle that appears to float on its nose is placed upon a hit or miss stripe background and framed by a monotone brown border. Circa 1940. 24" x 35". (Courtesy of Sylvia Giantonio)

Published by Schiffer Publishing, Ltd.
1469 Morstein Road
West Chester, Pennsylvania 19380
Please write for a free catalog.
This book may be purchased from the publisher.
Please include $2.00 postage.
Try your bookstore first.

We are interested in hearing from authors
with book ideas on related subjects.

Contents

Waldoboro Moo-Cow adapted from a note card and hooked by Elig Kay. Marked 89 [1989]. 25″ x 32″. (Courtesy of the Art Underfoot™ Treasury Collection)

Six o'clock in the morning, September 1990, the Brimfield Antiques Flea Market, Brimfield, Massachusetts. The Kents of Prince Edward Island, offer a wonderful selection of Canadian hooked rugs.

Acknowledgments

I wish to express my sincere gratitude to the many whose contributions made this book a reality. Involved in this undertaking were family members, friends and associates, rug hookers and teachers, antique dealers, shop, gallery and auction house owners, museums and institutions of learning. A special thank you to Nancy Schiffer for so graciously guiding this author through the steps of writing and publishing.

Kind acknowledgments to: Dot Abbott; Margaret Amdur; The St. Anthony Public Library, St. Anthony, Newfoundland; Art Underfoot™, Upper Montclair, New Jersey; Beauport, Sleeper-McCann House, Gloucester, Massachusetts; Benefit Street Gallery, Providence, Rhode Island; Margaret Bonning; Bristol Auctioneers, Wellesley, Massachusetts; Ann Cardoza; Max and Jessie Colbourne; Cathy Comins; Mary Ellen Cooper; Una Corriveau; Country Squire Antiques, Gorham, Maine; Crown and Eagle Antiques, New Hope, Pennsylvania; W. Cushing and Company, Kennebunkport, Maine; Jane Curtin; Patricia DeForest; Colette Donovan, Newburyport, Massachusetts; Catherine Duignan; The William Farnsworth Homestead-Farm, Waldoboro, Maine; The William A. Farnsworth Library and Art Museum, Rockland, Maine; Ferguson and D'Arruda Antiques; Jane McGown Flynn; Brenda Nichols-Gagne; Carol Garrity; Sylvia Giantonio, Newburyport, Massachusetts; Susan Goldberg; Emerson Greenaway; The Grenfell Handicrafts, St. Anthony, Newfoundland; The Sir Wilfred Thomason Grenfell Historical Society, St. Anthony, Newfoundland; The Grenfell House Museum, St. Anthony, Newfoundland; Heeltappers Antiques, Marblehead, Massachusetts; Harry W. and Barbara Hepburn; Hermitage Antiques, Harrison, Maine; The Hurricane Mat Hookers, St. Anthony, Newfoundland; Cindy and Paul Kaplan; S. H. Kearney; The Kent

Many behind-the-scenes efforts went into collecting and photographing hundreds of hooked rugs. Michael and Jamie work together to display this large rug still in the making.

Collection, Prince Edward Island, Canada; Pat and Connie Kent; Bob and Jean Kurtz; Meredith LeBeau; Marion B. MacConnell; R. Markowitz; Suzette McAvoy; Barbara and Robert Meltzer, New York City; Mary Louise Meyer; Robert and Joan Moshimer; Maria O'Brien, Marblehead, Massachusetts; Gwendolyn Packard; Ruth Pilgrim; Robert E. Richards Antiques, Bridge-water, Massachusetts; Ralph Ridolfino, Ocean City, New Jersey; Carol Roberts; Pat Ross; *Rug Hooking*, Harrisburg, Pennsylvania; Leah Christine Runci; Jane Sampson; Michael Santos; Olive Sauer; Stephen and Eleanor Score, Essex, Massachusetts; S. Segal; Sidney and Elizabeth Stewart; The Society for the Preservation of New England Antiquities, Boston, Massachusetts; Annie A. Spring; Danielle Swanson, Boxford, Massachusetts; The Collection of Sweet Nellie, New York City; Barbara Tarr; Eleanor E. Thompson; Florence and Anthony Travis; Lynn D. Trusdell; Evelyn N. Turbayne; James A. Turbayne; The Waldoboro Public Library, Waldoboro, Maine; Lynne Weaver Antiques, Wenham, Massachusetts; Wenham Cross Antiques, Boston, Massachusetts; Wenham Historical Association and Museum, Wenham, Massachusetts; D.C. Wolff.

Thank you to the following photographers: Kate Dooner; Linda Holt; Meredith LeBeau; Brenda Nichols-Gagne; Bob Kurtz; Douglas Congdon-Martin; Stacey Meltzer; Joan Moshimer; Robert Moshimer; and Michael Santos.

Rug measurements have been rounded to the nearest inch. Those hooked rugs, mats and related items to which no acknowledgement has been ascribed, belong to the author.

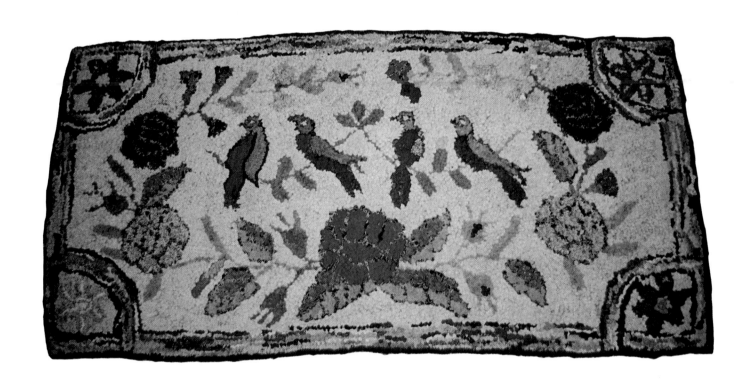

Four birds, all facing the same direction are perched on leafy twigs. Beneath and to the sides of the birds are sprays of flowers much like those seen on patterns. In contrast to their formal appearance, the rug hooker placed flowers of simple design in each corner. (Private Collection of Emerson Greenaway) (Photo by Jane Sampson)

Introduction

A visiting friend slowly scanned what used to be considered the living room of our home. Cautiously she made her way across the floor covered with hooked rugs piled three and four deep, then upon reaching an antique wing chair, rearranged a grouping of rolled hooked rugs in order to share the seat. She paused to catch her breath and seriously began to contemplate for a moment or two, what she saw. "Jessie", Florence stated, "you live and breathe hooked rugs." Her observation is true. Those that know me well will attest to the fact that I am surrounded by hooked rugs of all shapes and sizes; some that are whole and many more that are full of holes.

Close to twenty years ago my brother Jamie, antiques dealer and collector, suggested that I learn to repair hooked rugs. He felt that with this occupation I would always have work. He did not lie. Most unlike my usual demeanor, I listened, did what was suggested and learned to hook and repair rugs. Jamie's encouragement and guidance, lead to my collecting, buying and selling, teaching and speaking to interested groups. Though I never advertised, the restoration business steadily grew and eventually my mother, Evelyn was recruited to help with the mounting pile of repair work which found its way to my doors from all across the United States, England, and Canada. My children, Grace and Rob, have grown up with a mother whose wardrobe is adorned with odd bits of stray wool and burlap and whose cooking abilities include dyed wool and onion skin casseroles. In the early 1980s, Michael entered my life and I found a kindred soul, a person outside my family who truly understood my determination to restore and preserve hooked rugs that others would surely have tossed out. Michael has transported this author and thousands of hooked rugs throughout the United States and Canada. He carefully arranges the trips to St. Anthony,

My brother, Jamie, who suggested that I learn to repair hooked rugs, launched my career. He is pictured beside the rug he designed and is currently hooking.

Twin roses and morning glories rest upon a decorative
pedestal. Curlicue scrolls encircle the flowers. Circa 1880.
32" x 61". (Private Collection)

Newfoundland, so I am able to be among friends
and hook with the fine mat makers of the North.
Most recently he has safely brought me to the
special people in West Chester, Pennsylvania
who are publishing this book. For all of
Michael's love and efforts, I am forever grateful.

The purpose of this text is to allow readers the
opportunity to take a second look at the hooked
rugs that are today so popular with collector's;
to learn of the people that encouraged the
development and growth of the craft and to see
the many varieties of North American hooked
rugs. The chapters are filled with rugs of original
design and those that were hooked from patterns.

In the past, some collectors have suggested
that investing in hooked rugs crafted from
patterns is an unwise decision. An original
hooked scene, a one of a kind example of textile
folk art is to be treasured and valued as a piece of
art. But what of the Grenfell, Frost, and McGown
rugs, are they of less value? Of course not! Each
hooked mat and rug is a reflection of the person
who created it. Let's bestow high praises to the
unique rag and burlap rugs, but not be too hasty
in condemning those that were hooked from
stenciled patterns. Judge as you will, but fully
understand that each hooked rug, original in
design or hooked from a pattern, was
painstakingly worked by hand and heart.

Jessie A. Turbayne

A Historical Dilemma

Rug hooking was a craft born of necessity. The technique of pulling up or "hooking" rag strips and woolen yarns through a woven fabric base proved to be an economical and undemanding method of making floor coverings for drafty homes. The simplicity of the hooking process allowed rug makers the freedom to express their individual creativity. Hooked rugs were functional art, an art of need and poverty. Some controversy and mystery surround the origins of the craft. When and where rug hooking began can not be accurately documented, though theories abound.

W. W. Kent, author of a hooked rug trilogy, *The Hooked Rug*, 1930; *Rare Hooked Rugs*, 1941; *Hooked Rug Design*, 1949, uncovered evidence which lead him to believe an early form of hooking existed as far back as the sixth century. His theory was based upon examination of crude embroidery done by the Copts, descendants of the ancient Egyptians. These people worked wool yarns into raised loops using finely and coarsely woven cloth for a foundation. He noted that this skill, a supposed forerunner of modern rug hooking, was later brought into Spain by the Moors, Arabs, and Berbers.

After studying artifacts in Norway's Oslo Museum, Kent came to the conclusion that the ancestral roots of rug hooking could also be traced to the Scandinavian countries. When animal pelts were scarce, Kent believes the Bronze Age Vikings fashioned warm bed coverings from weavings and wool fibers using a skill similar to hooking. Many years have passed since Kent's three books were published. Some challenge his theories, citing the fact that the ancient textiles bore no relationship to hooked rugs. Opponents of Kent's findings strongly argue that rug hooking is a craft indigenous only to North America. Others are of the opinion that Kent was correct and believe that the roots of hooking run deeply into foreign cultures.

Evidence does exist, of a predecessor to rug hooking in nineteenth century Europe. During the early 1800s, the Yorkshire district of England was the center of a prosperous weaving industry.

A vessel of great size and importance, flying two British flags, cruises among sail boats and one diminutive ship; while on shore horses and oxen draw carts and their passengers. Possibly of Nova Scotia origins. 1900-1910. 17" x 36". (Courtesy of Heeltappers Antiques)

Mill workers and paupers collected and made use of the weavers' discarded ends, short leftover pieces of woolen yarn called "thrums". Hearth rugs and bed coverings were created by drawing the thrums through a cloth foundation. This process, referred to as "thrumming", was done by the common folk of England, Scotland, and Ireland. From these areas, as well as in France, came rugs that were "pegged, poked, brodded, and prodded". The names given to the rugs, the materials used, and the regions where they were made differed, but all bear a likeness to hooked rugs.

Around 1820, samples of jute, an inexpensive, natural fiber grown in India, were sent to Dundee, Scotland, renown for its linen production. After several years of experimenting with the fiber, the Scots perfected the process of weaving jute burlap. Soon the English began manufacturing the material in India; jute was plentiful and cheap and the Indian people worked for very low wages, thus drastically cutting the cost of production. The multipurpose burlap was a commodity much in demand throughout Europe, with profitable markets abroad.

Well into the 1850s, burlap, particularly in the form of sacking, was widely used in households across North America. Those of limited means, living in the northeast sea coast regions, had the need to create some sort of carpeting for drafty floors. Burlap feed and grain sacks made an ideal base for hooking rugs. The sacks were washed, cut, stretched and marked with designs. Prior to the introduction of burlap, some hooked rugs were worked upon homespun, linen, or canvas. Though durable as a base, it was difficult to pull rag strips through tightly woven cloth. The loose, open weave of the jute burlap made the task of hooking less tedious and not as time consuming. Burlap was a near perfect material to hook through; its use made the craft enjoyable. By the late 1870s, hooked rugs were common in the homes of America's northeast coastal areas and the Maritime Provinces of Canada. The craft thrived along the Atlantic shores where winters were long and cold. Women and the hardiest of farming and seafaring men, hooked mats and rugs. The craft was a pleasurable one, making snowbound hours pass quickly and providing warmth for the feet and a pleasing color for the eye. As the population traveled west, so did hooking. By the turn of the century, hooked rugs were being made across the United States and Canada.

Had the craft of rug hooking journeyed across the ocean with the peoples of Europe and Scandinavia when they came to start new lives in America and Canada? Or was rug hooking the product of North American ingenuity, a true American folk art? With no clear answer, the debate continues among those who wish to claim their country as the native homeland to rug hooking. Regardless of its ancestral background, the popularity of hooking rugs grew and flourished throughout Canada and the United States. The two neighboring countries share a heritage rich in the traditions of rug hooking. The many varieties of North American hooked rugs and the individuals who contributed to the history and development of the craft are the subjects of this book.

A home and garden of large pansies were the pride and joy of this rug hooker. By using the same color for the sky and interior of the window, the house appears to be hollow. A tear drop design forms a border. Dated 1897. (Photo Courtesy of Stephen and Eleanor Score)

The Varieties

Rugs were hooked in just about every shape and dimension. Those of scatter size and rectangular in nature were most plentiful, due in part to the convenience of using feed sacks as a base to hook through. A rectangular rug of small size could be hooked quickly and fit into a variety of household locations. Ambitious rug makers sewed together grain bags or pieces of burlap material to form foundations for room size rugs and lengthy stair runners. These projects of grand proportions required an abundance of rags to hook with and much time and patience. Rugs of half moon or semicircular shape fit well in front of doorways, hearth, and bedroom bureaus and chests. Less common were square and round rugs, for reasons unknown. Oblong styles were much in vogue during the 1930s and occasionally thereafter.

To make their rugs, hookers collected great quantities of rag, be it cotton, woolen yarns, flannel, homespun, canvas, paisley, velvet or other. The oldest hooked rugs were fashioned from what was worn, discarded, or available. Early rug hookers desiring a palette of colors extracted natural dyes by boiling fruits, vegetables, flowers, root, foliage, and whatever brought color change to the dye pot water. By the 1930s, wool was the widely preferred hooking material, it wore well, and could be used directly or dyed with commercially made products. Sold by the yard or pound, wool was available at notion stores and mill outlets. Those rug hookers of limited budget hunted for woolen clothing in thrift shops and at rummage sales.

A hooked rug shaped like the pansy it portrays. Circa 1940. 22'' x 23''.

A strong and bold portrait of a tri-colored dog. Background is horizontally hooked using a hit or miss variety of colors and fabrics. 1880-1890. 42'' x 46''. (Courtesy of Lynne Weaver Antiques)

Center rosettes add to the linear design of this geometric
pattern hooked with finely cut strips of wool during the
1940s. 35'' x 62''. (Private Collection)

14

Geometrics

Geometric designs were originally used by rug hookers as an exercise for the novice, an elementary lesson to teach and practice the craft of hooking. The beginner, possessing limited skills and a minimum of materials such as burlap, hook, and a grab bag of fabrics, could easily create a graphically pleasing floor covering. The only artistic talent required to plan a geometric pattern was the ability to draw a line or to trace an object such as a dinner plate onto a piece of burlap. This hand-drawn line, made easier still by following the burlap's weave, developed into squares, circles, triangles, and countless other shapes. As confidence grew, the designs developed into complex, repetitious patterns. With experience, and proper use of color, the rug maker could transform a flat square into a three dimensional box. By hooking the correct color combination, the illusion of height, width, and depth could be obtained on a flat piece of burlap. The geometric designs satisfied the basic needs of the beginner and yet offered a challenge to the skilled rug hooker.

Throughout their history, the majority of hooked rugs were made by women, though many men enjoyed the craft as a means of relaxation and as an avenue for expressing creativity. Seeing mothers, sisters, and wives happily working at their rug frames, men were often compelled to try their hand at this labor of love. Those reluctant to work with flowers and ornate scrolls were at ease designing and hooking graphic motifs. Sailors, during ocean voyages, often used idle time to hook rugs. Many fine examples were made at sea; geometric designs combined with nautical themes were most favored.

Many hookers of geometric rugs admired quilts and used quilt patterns as a source of inspiration when planning their rugs. The patterns intended for use as bed coverings adapted well as floor coverings. The burlap and rag imitations provided warmth and were pleasing to the eye. It was not uncommon to see a familiar quilt pattern, such as the Wedding Ring, Log Cabin, Tumbling Block, along with

The colorful inch squares on this rug appear to bulge from their burlap base. 1900-1920. 26" x 47". (Collection of Sidney and Elizabeth Stewart)

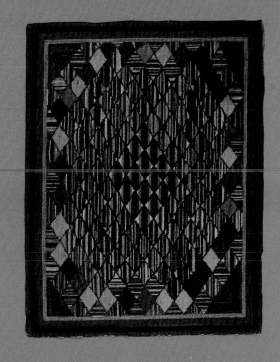

36" x 41".

31" x 40". (Private Collection)

38" x 60".

33" x 48". (Private Collection)

The above four rugs were hooked in New Hampshire by
one woman. Her skill at designing, use of color, and
proficiency at hooking are evident. Family records indicate
the rugs were most likely crafted between 1890 and 1910.

others, on the face of a hooked rug.

Due to its humble origins, hooked rugs of geometric designs were never considered to be of any great importance or value. Floral, or other "pretty" rugs, were protected from the wear and tear of constant foot traffic. Those of geometric design had earned the name of "work horse" of the hooked rug, due in part to the rug's participation in daily household chores. Relegated to the front of sinks and stoves, under the family pet, and at the door's threshold, this lowly rug served as a catch-all for drips and spills and was the resting place of wet and muddy shoes. When worn beyond repair, often the geometric rug's final chore was to act as a covering for the winter supply of firewood. Geometric hooked rugs were made in great numbers, and discarded in great numbers.

Multi-colored squares form changing optical patterns on this Canadian-made runner. 1910-1930. 34'' x 9'.

Detail view of the above runner. Hemp twine, woolen yarn, cotton rag and wool fabric were used by the hooker.

The owner of this simple geometric refers to it as his "snow on the window pane" rug. 1890-1910. 30'' x 63''. (Private Collection)

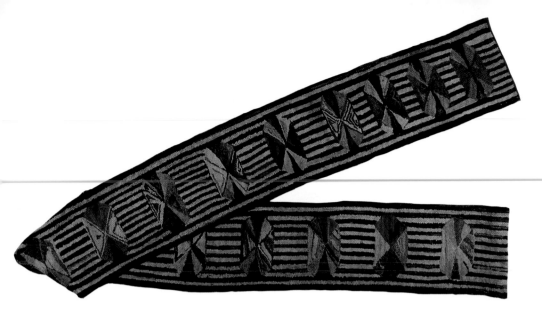

This early runner hooked on linen was created for a narrow stairway or hall. Its design is bold, graphic, and surprisingly modern looking. 1850-1870. 14'' x 14'. (Courtesy of Lynne Weaver Antiques)

An unusual geometric design rug, with motifs reminiscent of America's Southwest, was hooked by Thomas Carroll Hovey. Mr. Hovey was born in Dover, New Hampshire in 1855 and died in West Medford, Massachusetts in 1926. During his latter years, he was bedridden with Bright's disease; rug hooking occupied his days and nights. The grey and blue areas found throughout this rug were hooked using material from men's suits. 34'' x 67''.

Interwoven hooked stripes of color form a basket weave pattern. 1910-1920. 32'' x 70''. (Courtesy of the Benefit Street Gallery)

Today hooked rugs of geometric patterns are no longer considered unworthy, and antique examples are sought by a variety of collectors. Those who admire early country furniture find the simplicity of the designs appealing. Advocates of things contemporary are attracted to the hooked graphic themes that appear to defy time.

Diagonal bands cross a checkerboard background. Circa 1910. (Photo Courtesy of Stephen and Eleanor Score)

Hooked rugs of simple hit or miss stripes were often made using leftover material from other rugs. 1880-1900. 37'' x 72''. (Private Collection)

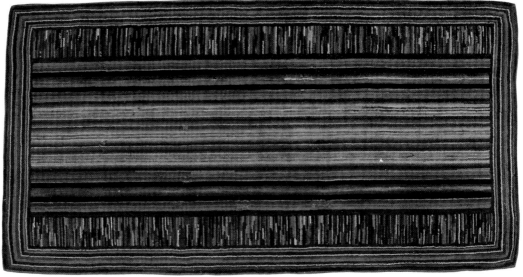

Oversized triangles of color, leafless vine with healthy red buds and off-centered double blossoms give this rug a child-like quality. Circa 1880-1890. 27'' x 60''. (Courtesy of Lynne Weaver Antiques)

Clam shell or lamb's tongue patterns were often drawn by tracing half of a small saucer or plate. A rug with its design heading in only one direction is indication it might have been made for a specific place. 1890-1910. 25'' x 68''.

Reminiscent of Art Deco design influence, circles and squares float on a field of navy blue. 1920-1930. 27'' x 47''. (Courtesy of Wenham Cross Antiques)

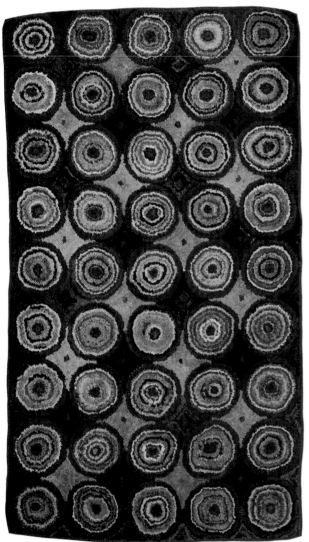

A pleasing rug of bold, graphic design. (Photo Courtesy of Stephen and Eleanor Score)

Concentric circles amidst dots and diamonds combine to form an optical illusion. Circa 1870. 37'' x 66''. (Private Collection)

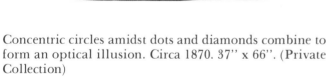

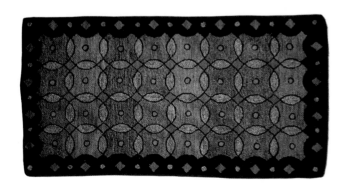

The double wedding ring quilt pattern was used when planning this hooked rug from Prince Edward Island. Circa 1930. 31'' x 60''.

The hexagonal star within a circle design, most likely copied from a quilt, makes a bold area-size rug. 1870-1880. 74'' x 76''. (Private Collection)

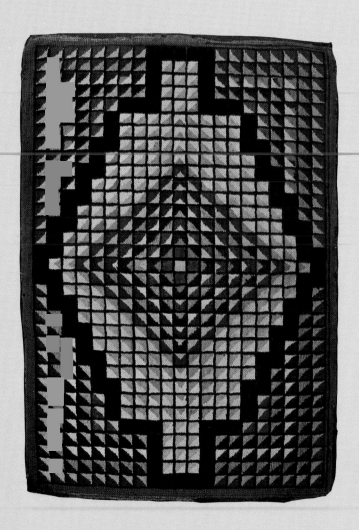

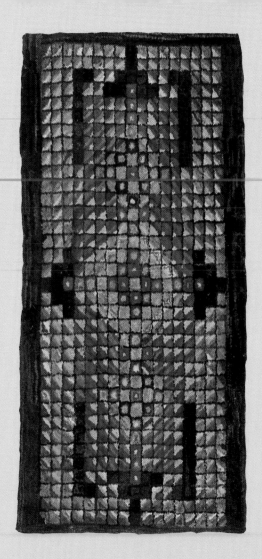

Inch blocks form two stepped pyramids with a multi-colored diamond center. 1900-1920. 29'' x 41''. (Private Collection)

A vibrant geometric pattern, this rug was hooked with many vintage fabrics. Of Maine origins. Circa 1900. 30'' x 64''. (Collection of R. Markowitz)

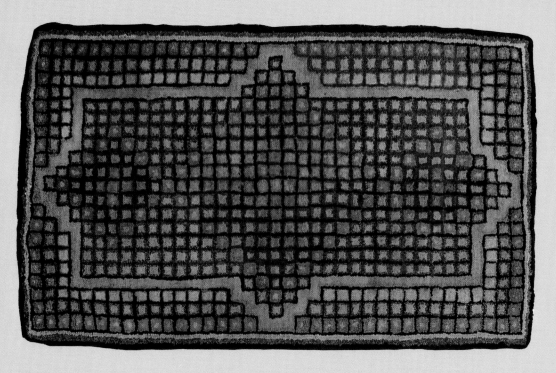

Hooked of monotone shades, this inch square or Boston side walk pattern was popular in the early 1900s. 1900-1920. 28'' x 48''. (Courtesy of Sylvia Giantonio)

Concentric rectangles frame a center scroll and peacock tail design. Braid was often sewn along the edges of hooked rugs to prevent or stop wear. 1880-1900. 35'' x 52''. (Private Collection)

Similar design as above, but with a more elaborate center. Believed to be of the same maker. 1880-1900. 28'' x 46''. (Private Collection)

Shades of pink, green and barn red combine in a radiating pattern. 1890-1910. 34'' x 39''. (Private Collection)

A project of grand proportion; this stair runner measures 30 feet in length. Circa 1940. 29'' x 30'.

Abstracts

In order to make rugs, hookers must collect large amounts of material. Baskets, boxes, and barrels are filled to capacity with rags of all shades and textures, wool plaids and tweeds, cotton calico, and swatches of prized paisleys. Once two or three rugs are completed, there remains a grab bag overflowing with small scraps. The frugal rug hooker utilizes these odd bits and pieces by producing a rug of abstract design. With no set description or idea to define the abstract rug, the hooker is free to create forms that are not easy to name or identify. Many rug makers find the artistic freedom to be a relaxing change from the types of rugs they usually work. The key to achieving a harmonious, finished product is to evenly distribute colors.

Abstract hooked rugs can not be associated with any particular era. They were made by early rug hookers and are still today, in vogue.

An all over abstract pattern is confined within a subdued border. Circa 1940. 22" x 48". (Courtesy of Wenham Cross Antiques)

Similar to a painting one might expect to find in the Museum of Modern Art, this hooked rug was designed and made by Bertie Lawrence of New York. Her materials included nylon stockings, unraveled lengths of knitted sweaters and fabric scraps. Circa 1970. (Private Collection)

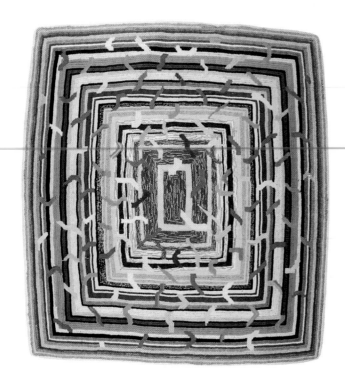

Concentric rectangles are the backdrop to countless "squigglely" lines that appear to float in space. Circa 1950. 38" x 41". (Courtesy of Wenham Cross Antiques)

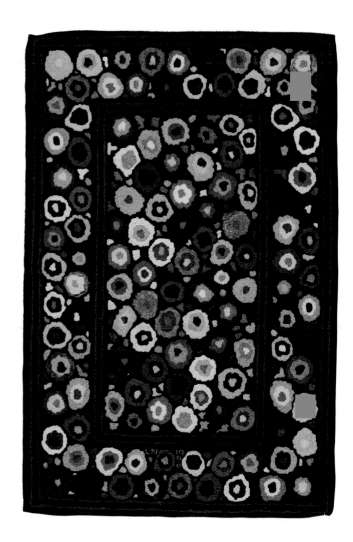

Mille Fleur, hooked by Lillian Nutting, designed by Jane McGown Flynn. 24" x 36". (Courtesy of the Art Underfoot™ Treasury Collection)

This colorful hooked rug combines geometric and abstract shapes. Circa 1940. 23" x 39". (Courtesy of Wenham Cross Antiques)

My brother Jamie's first attempt at hooking. Can you find the date 1978, that he hooked along one of the edges? 14'' x 14''.

This rug hooked of all wool, is reminiscent of a crazy quilt pattern. Often called broken glass design. Circa 1940. 39'' x 65''. (Private Collection)

Whirlpool, a Pearl McGown pattern, hooked with an abstract vision by Susan Goldberg. 24'' x 34''. (Photo courtesy of *Rug Hooking* magazine)

Artist, Susan Goldberg of Swampscott, Massachusetts began her painting career creating unique abstract designs on leather hides. The family owned leather finishing business utilized her talent by transforming the leather paintings into much in demand shoes and accessories for the home and office. By a chance whim, the young mother of two, enrolled in an adult education rug hooking course. With an immediate liking for this new medium, burlap became Susan's canvas and she began to hook her abstract designs with a palette of rainbow colored wool strips. Susan is an active and prominent member of today's rug hooking community. She is an accredited McGown teacher, writes and does extensive research on the craft and continues to inspire other rug hookers with her wool and burlap "escapes" from realism.

Close-up of *Whirlpool.* (Photo courtesy of *Rug Hooking*)

Abstract #1, original design by Susan Goldberg. 33'' x 38''. (Photo courtesy of *Rug Hooking* magazine)

Close-up of *Abstract #1*. (Photo courtesy of *Rug Hooking*)

Close-up of hooked abstract, right. (Photo courtesy of *Rug Hooking* magazine)

An original, untitled abstract by Susan Goldberg. 19'' x 63''. (Photo courtesy of *Rug Hooking*)

Free form lines of rainbow color create a border for a kaleidoscope garden of blooms and foliage. Behind is a background appearing as a water color wash. As the garden grew, the rug hooker failed to continue the clam shell edging, stopping its path abruptly. 1880-1890. 34'' x 65''. (Private Collection)

Flowers of Rag

Thanks to art, instead of seeing a single world, our own, we see it multiply until we have before us as many worlds as there are original artists.

Marcel Proust

Ask rug makers to hook a flower and the interpretations will be more numerous and varied than the buds that bloom each spring. The hooked leaves, stems, and petals differ, as do the people who conceive them. The variety of flowers hooked of rag multiply and grow into a garden, bursting with color and never wilting with the changing of the seasons.

Women and men attempted to draw on burlap grain sacks and then hook the image of the plants that grew in yards, fields, and forests. When artistic ability failed to create realism, imaginations took flight. Many unique and often whimsical blossoms appeared on hooked rugs, the likes of which have never been seen in nature by the most scholarly botanist. The awaited delivery of seed catalogs further expanded the rug hookers' horticultural horizons, bringing into the home unknown flora and fauna to enjoy and copy. Commercial pattern makers, beginning with E. S. Frost in the late 1860s, produced the stamped outline of true-to-life floral bouquets on burlap. Similar to the pages of a child's coloring book, the burlap needed only to be hooked with the appropriate hues to achieve a likeness to Mother Nature's own flower bed. Though the finished rug was not always a mirror image of the flower desired, the results were none-the-less charming.

In addition to brightening a room's decor, floral hooked rugs were made in honor of special occasions, often accompanying the recipient from cradle to coffin. Keepsake pieces, decorated with bud and bloom, name, and date of birth, were hooked to mark the arrival of a daughter, niece, or grand-daughter. Church runners and altar rugs, the majority of which

Wind blown flowers and their leaves dance across a subtle field. Some of the floral artwork dares to leave the confines of the picture and rests atop the thin line frame. Hooked on homespun. 1860-1880. 36" x 76". (Courtesy of Colette Donovan)

were floral patterns, were lovingly crafted by hand for the bride's walk down the aisle. Such events were times of joy, recorded on burlap by the artist's hook. When fresh floral arrangements were unavailable due to the ice and snow of winter, flowers hooked of rag draped the casket of the deceased. These hooked blankets were known as coffin rugs.

Whether a simple posy of four rounded petals with a button size splash of color in the center, or a meticulously formed cabbage rose with twelve shades of crimson, each floral hooked rug was unique and became the maker's personal garden of creativity.

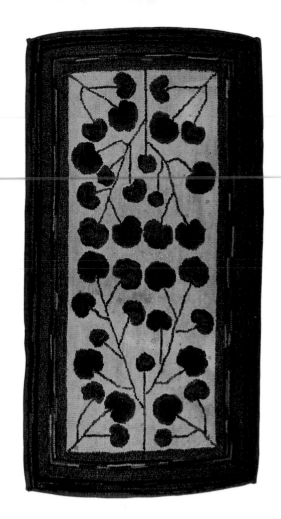

A cheerful display of geraniums and leaves. Made in New Hampshire. 1900-1920. 22" x 45". (Private Collection)

Twisting and turning blue scroll competes for space by partially obscuring the large mustard colored flowers that burst from the center bouquet. Patches of grey tweeds and hit or miss lines complete a busy background. 1890-1910. 37" x 70". (Collection of Sidney and Elizabeth Stewart)

A hooked rug of simple design. Circa 1900. 34'' x 36''. (Private Collection)

Single tree-like stalk of rose hips, blooms and leaves fills this hooked study. Concentric lines of solid and tweed fabrics form the frame. 1880-1900. 31'' x 59''. (Courtesy of Lynne Weaver Antiques)

A delicate garland of flowers is the sole subject of this hooked rug. Colors used in the wreath are repeated on the rug's edges. 1860-1880. 43'' x 72''. (Private Collection)

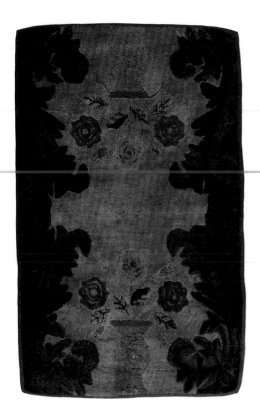

A pair of urns in mirror-like symmetry grace the ends of this early hooked rug. A single raised and sculptured rose decorates each container. Center ground was hooked from cotton and linen rag, border scrolls and edges a mixture of brown wools and cotton rag. 1860-1880. 29'' x 47''. (Private Collection)

Twin cornucopia of vibrant blues overflow with an abundance of flowers. A simple looped line oval and a jagged red scroll encompass the expertly planned and hooked center; indicating that perhaps the rug had more than one maker. A background of pale color, interrupted by lines of a darker shade, creates its own interest. Circa 1880. 43'' x 73''.

A diminutive table rug hooked with strips of silk on a homespun foundation. 1880-1900. 14'' x 24''. (Courtesy of Colette Donovan)

An overflowing bouquet of summer flowers spills out of a tipped wicker basket. Border leaves of autumn color speak of yet another season. Circa 1880.

This hooked rug has qualities of a Van Gogh painting. A wreath of bright blossoms and buds swirls among fronds of green. Meandering lines of every shade of grey keep the movement of the rug alive. Circa 1930. 33'' x 68''.

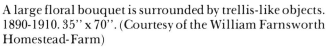

A large floral bouquet is surrounded by trellis-like objects. 1890-1910. 35'' x 70''. (Courtesy of the William Farnsworth Homestead-Farm)

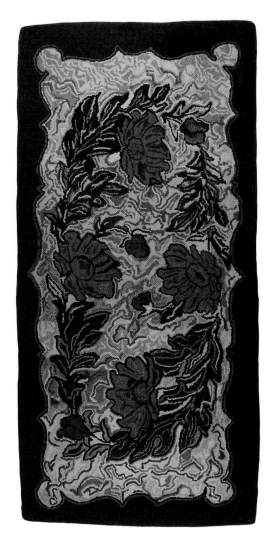

Oak leaves and acorns are placed in the corners of this well designed floral rug. Circa 1880. 44'' x 52''. (Private Collection)

Carefully shaded roses, calla lilies, jonquils and iris create a center for this oval hooked rug. Circa 1940. 33'' x 57''. (Courtesy of Charles and Evelyn Turbayne)

Grand scale feather plumes join with bursting peony blossoms to create a hooked rug that would be the focal point of any room. Hooked from a pattern; designer unknown. Circa 1940. 7'6'' x 9'5''.

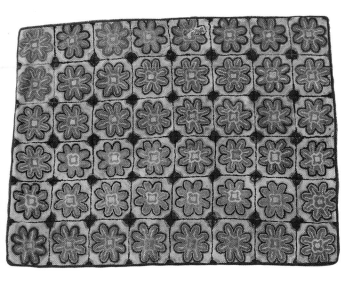

A simple posy repeated 48 times makes for a hooked rug of area size. 1890-1910. 52'' x 70''.

A perfectly arranged nosegay is framed by feather-like scrolls and corner pieces. Muted tones appear throughout the rug. 1880-1900. 32'' x 50''. (Private Collection)

The maker of this rug utilized a playing card design to showcase flowers, leaves and simple scrolls. 1890-1910. 40'' x 57''. (Private Collection)

38

Opposite page:
A jungle-like growth of leaves, ferns, and scrolls fills this vibrant rug. Hooked mainly of woolen yarns. Circa 1930. 37'' x 70''. (Private Collection)

Opposite page bottom:
This floral hooked rug accompanied Mr. Sidney Stewart on his New England lecture tours. He was able to identify all but one of the hooked flowers. When questioning the maker as to the variety she intended, her reply, "The unidentifiable flowers are blue bells, but being an individualist, I hooked them red." Circa 1940. 25'' x 46''. (Collection of Sidney and Elizabeth Stewart)

This page right:
A dozen open roses, hooked of delicate shades, fade in the presence of a scroll of vibrant blues. The colors of the red roses and brown leaves are echoed in the border. Circa 1880. 27'' x 48''. (Courtesy of the William Farnsworth Homestead-Farm)

The mirrored image of the twin red flowers is broken by the random placement of the surrounding buds and leaves. Two tri-color ropes twist their way around the border. The rug hooker confused the path of the rope in two corners. Circa 1890. 37'' x 64''. (Collection of Sidney and Elizabeth Stewart)

Corner and center designs composed of joining hearts share a dark, mottled field with a cluster of flowers. A variety of different blooms, buds and leaves thrive on a single stem. 1870-1890. 31'' x 56''. (Courtesy of the William Farnsworth Homestead-Farm)

Paul Revere swiftly rides, warning of the British approach. The spire of Old North Church is visible in the upper left corner. Bushes and grass blend into a wave of green and off-white lines. 1940-1950. 24" x 36". (Courtesy of D.C. Wolff)

Familiar Faces and Places

Most antique hooked rugs do not come with histories. Old rugs bear few clues as to their makers' identities. We can only guess the personality and lifestyle of the individual, who long ago, hooked the rug we now treasure. By studying the handiwork, we are able to determine the rug maker's proficiency at hooking and we can presume to know the artist's preference for colors. From careful examination of the fabrics and observation of wear, we can approximate the rug's age, but not that of its creator. Rugs that were neither signed nor dated by their makers, passed through many hands and traveled many miles. The creators of this underfoot art, remain anonymous. Few collectors will ever know who is responsible for hooking the antique rugs that are bought and sold in shops and at auction.

Those rugs of original, one of a kind design, that featured people, animals, and houses, are the most sought after of all hooked rugs. Sentimental rug makers were often compelled to depict, through the medium of hooking, the things in their lives that were near and dear. Such projects were carefully planned in the mind and heart of the rug hooker and then sketched by hand upon an available backing, such as burlap, homespun, or discarded grain sack. As the rug maker worked to hook strips of rag into recognizable subjects, family members became involved by voicing opinions on the artist's portrayal of familiar faces and places. The completed rug became a source of pride and joy for the rug hooker and members of the household. Many had contributed to make this special rug a true labor of love.

The emotions expressed through the craft of hooking were not always those of endearment and respect. During times of personal strife, hooked rugs were a means of venting distaste, frustration, jealousy, and an assortment of other emotional maladies. Rugs intended to mock the likes of drunkards, unfaithful husbands, and dreaded relatives were called scorn or spite rugs. What great satisfaction an angered family member must have felt when hooking the image of a disliked relative; knowing that before long, the completed rug would be placed upon the floor for all to wipe their dirty shoes upon. This rug served as a silent but sweet revenge for shabby treatment.

The rag portraits and still lifes of the faces and places familiar to the rug hooker give us a brief, but often informative glimpse of the artist's world. Though the majority of questions concerning the person who crafted the rug will forever remain unanswered, our curiosity is for the moment subdued by the bits and pieces of personal information found hooked in these rag vignettes.

The reason for bestowing abundant praises and high price tags on this special category of hooked rugs is twofold. Rugs of homemade design, picturing unique subjects, are valued as original works of art. And of all hooked rugs, only those that depict scenes from life can grant us the insight to imagine the person who toiled at the rug frame.

Hooked by a loving son or daughter. 1920-1930. (Private Collection of Emerson Greenaway) (Photo by Jane Sampson)

A pattern possibly copied from a rug sold by Ralph Burnham, entitled *Boy Franklin in Philadelphia*. Young Ben, carrying a package under his arm, strolls the street. The use of differing colors and materials forms an abstract patchwork pattern on the road. Tweed material was used to hook the cobblestone sidewalk. Circa 1930-1950. (Private Collection of Emerson Greenaway) (Photo by Jane Sampson)

42

A gentleman in the gutter lies
His face upturned to starlite skies
A helping hand—A word of cheer
Would dissipate the fumes of beer
The fumes of rum—The fumes of
     wine
That caused this man to lay supine

Large hooked stars, wavy lines and shapes are backdrop for this poor befuddled fellow. 1900-1920. 36" x 49". (Courtesy of Ralph Ridolfino)

A patriotic rug hooker illustrates a stout Union soldier at guard with waving flag. To appear as if rippling in the wind, the rug maker alternated Old Glory's stripes forming a crude checkerboard field. Dated 1862. (Photo Courtesy of Stephen and Eleanor Score)

Wind swept sky is a background to two young skaters, bundled up against the cold. Pond and sky were cropped to form a frame for this winter scene. Circa 1900. (Photo Courtesy of Stephen and Eleanor Score)

43

Two black men with floating hats pose beside a large center star and simple border of three flowering stems. Early 20th century. 35'' x 42''. (Courtesy of Harry W. and Barbara Hepburn)

Two black women dressed in similar outfits are portrayed in a summer garden, complete with butterflies in flight. Early 20th century. 29'' x 45''. (Courtesy of Harry W. and Barbara Hepburn)

La Recherche, copyright Roslyn Logsdon. 1983. 22'' x 34''. (Courtesy of the Art Underfoot™ Treasury Collection)

Hooked by Dot Abbott from a pattern, this antique shop scene includes, at bottom left, a hooked rug still on its frame. 24'' x 28''. (Courtesy of Dot Abbott)

Quai D' Anjou, copyright Roslyn Logsdon 1984. 30'' x 36''. (Courtesy of the Art Underfoot™ Treasury Collection)

A farm house, equipped with an extremely large glass paneled front door and two first floor windows, sits beside a barn in this tranquil country scene. A single line of hooking carefully spaced creates a simple fence. A border hooked with tweeds and solid hit or miss colors frames the scene. Dated 1895. (Photo Courtesy of Stephen and Eleanor Score)

Small table top mats were hooked by many Canadians during the long winters, and made available to visiting tourists on summer excursions.

Mats of this small size were sold as coasters. Circa 1940. 3" x 3".

On the left, two tiny houses and foreground fence are almost lost amidst the snow. Circa 1940. 3" x 4". On the right, a church hooked of not so fine strips is framed by two rows of blue hooked yarn. Circa 1930. 4" x 4".

A man who appears to be carrying an arm load of fire wood walks over the snow to his home. Hooked from cotton knit jersey. Circa 1940. 10" x 12". (Courtesy of Florence Travis)

This simple winter setting of house, shed, tree and fence was hooked from rayon and cotton jersey. Circa 1940. 5'' x 8''. (Courtesy of Florence Travis)

A typical winter scene, however the stream does not flow under the bridge and on its course appears to flood the house. Rug hooker was obviously enjoying her hooking and disregarded the placement of colors. Circa 1940. 10'' x 12''.

Two hunters dressed in brightly checked jackets are surprised by a deer outside their cabin door. Note that the hunter taking aim was able to don only one snowshoe. Most likely of Canadian origins. Circa 1930. 18'' x 36''. (Private Collection of S.H. Kearney)

A small house with three chimneys beckons you to its doors via two separate paths. Both the sky and foreground employ horizontal hooking with strips of appropriate color. Circa 1910. 18'' x 38''.

Rug hooker, Patricia DeForest, chose to depict her 1750 antique home using burlap as her canvas and strips of wool as her paint. 1985. 27'' x 38''. (Courtesy of Patricia DeForest) (Photo by Bob Kurtz)

This rug documents the old and new Confederation Building in Charlottetown, Prince Edward Island. The stark modern building, built in 1964 to commemorate Canada's entering the Confederation, houses an art gallery, theatre, library, etc. Rug maker used a very limited palette, but produced a unique rug. Prince Edward Island made. 26'' x 53''.

An unembellished home and an unusual spear-like striped tree rest upon a vertically hooked striated field. 19th century. (Photo Courtesy of Stephen and Eleanor Score)

A border of faces with changing expression surround a grouping of Christmas toys. 1920-1930. (Photo Courtesy of Stephen and Eleanor Score)

A Currier and Ives scene hooked by friend and fellow rug hooker, Dot Abbott. 31'' x 43''. (Courtesy of Dot Abbott)

Many Canadian rug makers hook in straight horizontal lines. Americans hook in a random fashion, some lines, some curves. This winter scene of mill, horse, sleigh and cow is vertically hooked. Most noticeable in the sky, you can see the lines of hooking run up and down, not side to side as is commonly done. 1960-1970. 25'' x 38''. (Private Collection of S. Segal)

This winter scene is the hooked version of a painting by Tromblé. Women from Quebec were hired by the artist to dye yarns to match the colors found in his painting, then hook a likeness of the work. Purchased in Quebec during the 1940s for $125. 29'' x 37''. (Collection of Charles and Evelyn Turbayne)

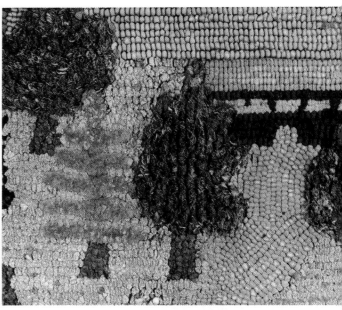

An unusual night scene indicated by the front window shades of the house being partially drawn and emitting interior light. Male and female moose come out to eat fallen apples. Looking closely under the trees and on the open field, you see specks of red fabric which represent the grounded fruit. A stream, of the same color as the foreground and background, is visible due to the interruption in the horizontal hooking path of the field. The water meanders past the house en route to a saw mill or to pass under a covered bridge. Cut lengths of wood and visible tree stumps suggest a lumberjack dwells in the cabin. 1890-1910. Possibly of Canadian origins. 27'' x 34''.

Close-up of above rug. Many of the trees were hooked with sisal, raised and sculptured. Upon close examination they resemble and have the texture of scrub brushes.

Two ground hogs nibble at a garden goodie. Circa 1930. 20'' x 35''. (Courtesy of Colette Donovan)

Fox with white tipped tail stares through beady little eyes. Rug hooker felt the frame and borders were of equal importance to the centered fox. Early 20th century. (Photo Courtesy of Stephen and Eleanor Score)

Perfectly posed Siamese cat with long whiskers and parted hair is placed amidst a background of solid color and striped diamonds. 1890-1910. 31'' x 52''. (Collection of Sidney and Elizabeth Stewart)

Close up of a forlorn face with red nose, fur on his or her head neatly parted.

A hooked memorial to Tommy the cat, shows him at play within the confines of a fenced yard. Flowers and hit or miss striped blocks frame his image. Dated June 2, 1936-July 2, 1941, the length of Tommy's life. 46'' x 60''. (Courtesy of Ferguson and D'Arruda Antiques)

Hollow eyed cat is framed by sprigs of ivy and paired shamrocks. Early 20th century. (Photo Courtesy of Stephen and Eleanor Score)

Never-Never Rug hooked by Jane Curtin from a pattern. Possibly a copy of an early rug which passed through Ralph Burnham's Ipswich, Massachusetts Trading Post in the early part of the 1900s. 31'' x 64''. (Courtesy of Jane Curtin)

A pet family portrait of Kit, for Kitty; Coq, the French word for chicken; and Hope, the dog. Perhaps Kit was a later addition to the trio, indicated by her smaller size and cramped sideways position. A very scrawny tree separates Coq and Hope. Simple five petal flowers border the animals. Circa 1890. (Photo courtesy of Brenda Nichols-Gagne)

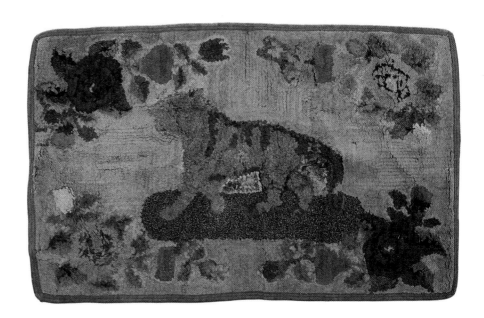

A tiger posed on a carpet of blue is surrounded by corners of roses in full bloom and buds of pink, red, white, and blue. Circa 1880. 20'' x 32''. (Courtesy of the William Farnsworth Homestead-Farm)

53

A perched eagle of simple form and little detail is the centerpiece of this composition. On either side are designs reminiscent of pieces of scroll work. The backdrop is of irregular rectangular shapes. Early 20th century. (Photo Courtesy of Stephen and Eleanor Score)

Bright solid areas of color compose a portrait of two puffins. The gentleman rug maker hooked the blue areas with acrylic yarn and the rest with strips cut from nylon tights. The technique of horizontal hooking was used. Made in Newfoundland. 1990. 29'' x 30''.

A proud peacock struts across a plain background. Rug hooker carefully detailed the eyes of the bird's feathers and balanced the composition with a grouping of flowers in the bottom corner. Early 20th century. (Photo courtesy of Stephen and Eleanor Score)

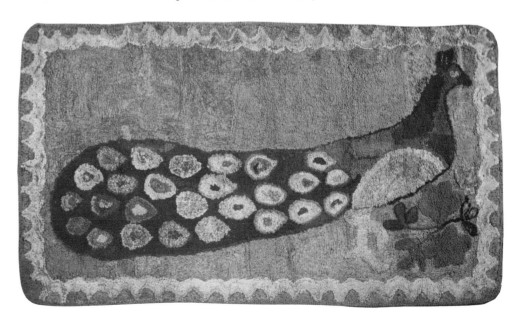

Patricia DeForest holds the rug she is currently hooking, *The King*, a design by Marion Hamm. Instructor Marion MacConnell looks on. (Photo by Bob Kurtz)

A pair of blue eyed sea gulls stroll toward an unknown yellow object, perhaps a dish of food. The foreground as well as the sky is horizontally hooked from various colors and types of rag. A brown hit or miss frame completes the picture. Circa 1910. 31'' x 43''. (Private Collection)

Rooster and hen are face to face on a patch work background. The inwardly directed objects are likely fence posts or crude shamrocks. Early 20th century. (Photo Courtesy of Stephen and Eleanor Score)

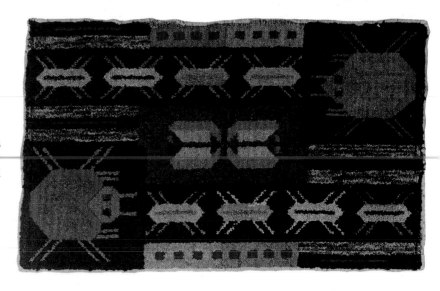

A regiment of bugs crawl in line across this unusual rug. Rarely were insects portrayed by rug hookers. Hooked by Thomas Carroll Hovey in the 1920s. 24" x 40".

Far Side Cows, copyright Denise Fondren 1990. 34" x 57". (Courtesy of the Art Underfoot™ Treasury Collection)

Quilt II, Cow I copyright Tish Murphy 1989. 33" x 44". (Courtesy of the Art Underfoot™ Treasury Collection)

Dressed in their Sunday best, Mrs. Rabbit and her son, Peter, run up the garden path. A rug to delight any young child. 1910-1920. 30'' x 47''. (Courtesy of Lynne Weaver Antiques)

Inspiration for the hooked rug.

A treasured Christmas gift presented to the author by a dear friend and fellow rug hooker, Jane Curtin. The parade of Dedham Pottery rabbits are hooked to form a neat border. Marked 88 [1988]. 20'' x 30''.

The *Iowa* remains tied up at dock while oversized birds dive bomb into the water. Simple, yet grand scroll frames the scene. Circa 1900. 34'' x 74''. (Courtesy of the William Farnsworth Homestead-Farm)

A woman from Newfoundland hooked this polar bear floating past an iceberg from strips of stretchy nylon material. Sky and clouds crafted from hand dyed panty hose. 1990. 18'' x 39''. (Courtesy of Bristol Auctioneers)

A ghost-like outline of a ship sails straight into an under sized sail boat. The rug maker perhaps copied the ships from printed patterns and placed their images randomly on burlap. 1920-1930. 28'' x 46''. (Courtesy of the William Farnsworth Homestead-Farm)

Heading for harbor, under full sail, the rear flag identifies this ship as American. The rug maker expertly captures the movement of the water. From a pre-printed pattern. Circa 1920. 36'' x 69''. (Courtesy of the William Farnsworth Homestead-Farm)

Same pattern as above, but different in size and use of color. Circa 1920. 28'' x 36'' (Courtesy of the William Farnsworth Homestead-Farm)

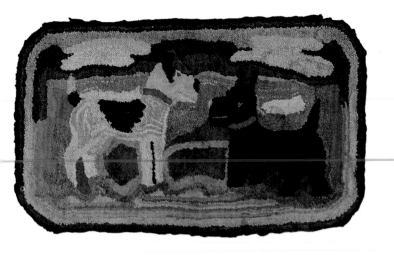

A friendly confrontation between two small dogs. Background field and sky were created by hooking broad areas of color. 1920-1930. 27" x 46". (Courtesy of Lynne Weaver Antiques)

The rug hooker outlined this dark crouching dog with waves of color before finishing a more subdued background. Circa 1880. (Photo Courtesy of Stephen and Eleanor Score)

Two dogs rest on a field of varying browns, with a single patch of make-do blues. A simple vine with leaves and ball-like flowers frame the duo. Further decoration of a scalloped wool edge was carefully sewn in place. Circa 1870-1880. 27" x 59". (Courtesy of Colette Donovan)

A beloved white dog is honored and placed inside a wreath of flowers, leaves and grapes. The portrait is further enhanced by an ornate border. Note varying patches of background color. Circa 1870. 29'' x 53''. (Collection of Sidney and Elizabeth Stewart)

Though a dog of simple shape and color, the rug hooker accurately placed markings unique to this pet. Note the vivid blues of the grapes.

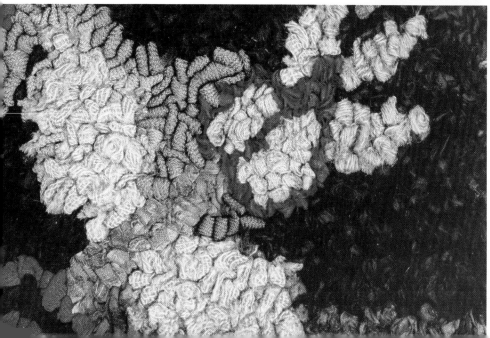

Extreme close up shows the variety of textures found in this rug.

A frisky puppy with similar markings follows its mother. Large, crudely drawn scroll with a red vein-like line frames the pair. 1890-1910. (Photo Courtesy of Stephen and Eleanor Score)

Solid dark rectangles and an oval of hit or miss stripes encompass the simple figure of a dog. (Photo Courtesy of Stephen and Eleanor Score)

Portrayed within an overpowering frame is a tiny horse with its name "Jess" divided and printed boldly on either side of its owner. The scroll frame and overly large corner designs were likely copied from a pattern. The rug hooker randomly interjected differing shades of brown to the background, creating interest in an otherwise plain field. Circa 1880. 24" x 46". (Private Collection of S.H. Kearney)

A swiftly running stallion with wind in its mane and tail is similar to a horse silhouette used for weather vanes. Eye-catching circles with inner triangles appear to roll with the movement of the horse. 19th century. (Photo Courtesy of Stephen and Eleanor Score)

The figure of a horse named "Smuggler" trots in a center rectangle. A wide border of abstract shapes nearly obscures a fine vine of small flowers and leaves. 19th century. (Photo Courtesy of Stephen and Eleanor Score)

Two simply drawn and outlined horses create a scene with child-like qualities. Perhaps this was the work of a young rug hooker. 20th century. 14" x 32". (Courtesy of Ralph Ridolfino)

Gwendolyn Packard, member of a Massachusetts hooking group, works at completing "Soumac Medallion", designed by Jane McGown Flynn. A woven Oriental rests beneath her feet. 1990. (Photo Courtesy of Bob Kurtz)

Faux Orientals

As the United States slowly recovered from the Civil War, people's spirits lifted, personal riches grew, and homes were embellished with finery to attest new found prosperity. Conforming with popular decorating trends, some rug hookers wanted a more formal appearance in the rugs they made. Many admired the imported, hand-knotted Oriental carpets that graced the grand mansions of the wealthy, but few could afford the genuine article in their own houses.

Oriental carpets became a source of inspiration for scores of rug hookers and small businesses that printed burlap patterns. The E.S. Frost and Company's hooked rug pattern collection of the 1870s offered a group of "Turkish" treasures. Some of the patterns were detailed copies of authentic Oriental carpets while others in the collection featured designs reminiscent of the American Indian. The Frost stenciled Turkish burlaps varied in size from an area rug of 72" x 108" to a chair seat design measuring 14¾" x 20¾". As the demand for the Oriental copies increased and time proved them to be a profitable market, other pattern manufacturers offered their rug hooking audiences a variety of Oriental, Turkish, and Persian interpretations.

Color schemes similar to those of true Oriental carpets could be achieved by dyeing pieces of wool fabric. Varying shades of terra cotta red, earthen brown, natural ivory, and a palette of other mellow colors were used to hook the intricate medallions and symbols decorating the rug's field and borders. To create a velvety sheen, rug hookers often clipped or cut off the tops of the hooked loops. The results were lustrous. To the untrained eye, a hooked Oriental imitator could successfully masquerade as the real thing.

Rug hookers, preferring not to use commercially printed patterns, made their own designs by copying the motifs woven into the bona fide carpeting. The foreign designs were easily adapted to suit the rug hooker's needs. By

Finely executed Oriental mat hooked in Rhode Island. 1950-1970. 24" x 45".

increasing or decreasing the figures used in borders, the rug could be hooked to measure any needed size. Not all hookers chose color combinations appropriate for creating true Oriental reproductions. Whether a desire to be unique or a lack of proper dyes, the unpredictable use of colors helped produce a finished rug that was surprising and fresh.

As a tribute to the finely woven works of art imported from the Middle East and Asia, North American rug hookers created their hooked version of the Oriental carpet. Imitation, they say, is the most sincere form of flattery.

The popular Frost Turkish Pattern #108. Hooking with strips ½" wide or more, accounts for a rug displaying less clear and accurate detail. Origins unknown. Circa 1910. 36" x 70". (Private collection of S.H. Kearney)

Frost Turkish Pattern #108 in need of repair, but of unusual and pleasing color combinations. Maine origins. 1930-1940. 38" x 72".

An Oriental runner of unusual color combination was hooked by a Massachusetts husband and wife team during the 1950s. Initials of each are hooked at opposite ends of the pattern. 30'' x 85''. (Private Collection)

This fine start of a hooked Oriental runner was rescued from the town dump.

The same husband and wife hookers crafted an additional runner in the 1950s. Note that this pattern is identical to the unfinished runner rescued from the dump, left. 29'' x 105''. (Private Collection)

67

"Peking" a Chinese inspired design from an Heirloom pattern is newly hooked by Doris LaPlante. 45'' x 72''. (Courtesy of the Art Underfoot™ Treasury Collection)

"Peking" hooked by Jane Curtin. 45'' x 72''. (Courtesy of Jane Curtin)

Frost Turkish Pattern #132 is reminiscent of tribal weavings. Origins unknown. Circa 1910. 26'' x 45''.

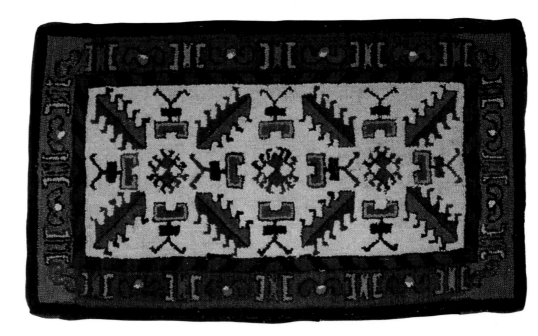

Intricate designs dominate this finely hooked Persian-style area rug. 1950-1970. 52'' x 64''. (Courtesy of Ferguson and D'Arruda Antiques)

"Song of Persia", designed by Jane McGown Flynn was recently hooked by Evelyn Wood, 36'' x 60''. (Courtesy of the Art Underfoot™ Treasury Collection)

An exceptional example of a Waldoboro rug. Oval floral and foliage wreaths were often set against a dark background. Initials were likely those of the maker or recipient of this handsome piece. Though many functioned strictly as decorative objects, this rug shows signs of wear from foot traffic. Circa 1870. 36'' x 70''. (Collection of Danielle Swanson)

The Motivators

Waldoboro

The German immigrants who settled in the ship building community of Waldoboro, Maine were responsible for hooking rugs of raised and sculptured designs. The majority of the finest rugs crafted between 1860 and 1880 depicted colorful floral wreaths and bouquets with borders of scrolls or flowers and foliage. Bunches of purple grapes often appeared as well as a centered figure of a dog or cat. Some earlier examples hooked on linen still exist.

The technique of "hoving up" or raising the pile of a rug to varying heights is reminiscent of the deep sculptured carpets of Germany, Holland, and France. German weavers also originated a method of raising figures on their woven coverlets. Exposure to the three dimensional textiles of native lands, most likely inspired the Waldoboro rug makers to create their own versions with hook, grain sack, and rag. Canadians of French descent made raised and sculpted hooked rugs, but of more varied designs.

During the 1920s and early 1930s Warren Weston Creamer, proprietor of a fine antique shop in Waldoboro's Reed Mansion, sold many of the old, locally crafted rugs, while Ralph Burnham offered the sculptured works of art in his Ipswich, Massachusetts' Trading Post.

Today hooked rugs with raised motifs are referred to as Waldoboro type or style rugs, regardless of their origins. Due to the extremes in the height of the pile, in some examples up to 3", the raised hooked rugs served more of a decorative purpose than that of a functional one. Though scarce, this accounts for the good condition of many of the old "Waldoboros" seen today.

From Burnham's Antique Trading Post, Ipswich, Massachusetts, an interior view featuring an early Waldoboro rug (1860-1880) with greatly raised floral design center and corner scrolls. Photograph 1905-1930. (Courtesy of Annie A. Spring)

Sculptured and raised roses, singular bunch of grapes, buds and blooms grace this Waldoboro-made rug. Circa 1885. 27" x 48". (Courtesy of The William Farnsworth Homestead-Farm)

The unusually large size of this rug required that it be photographed from a second story roof. Background was hooked using balls of hemp twine, instead of the usual rag strips. The long unbroken twine lengths enabled the rug maker to hook nonstop for longer periods of time. Flowers in center oval and forming wreath are raised and hooked of mixed materials. Circa 1890. 103" x 139". Possibly made in Northern Maine or Canada. (Courtesy of Colette Donovan)

Primitive looking raised grapes, blossoms, and leaves grow on stalk-like stems, framed by a simple border. Origins unknown. Circa 1890. 31'' x 46'. (Private Collection)

Background of this area rug is hooked from unbleached cotton and linen rag. The vines and floral outline are hooked of twine; the raised flowers and buds hooked of rag and woolen yarn. Origins unknown, purchased in Connecticut, but of Waldoboro style. Circa 1880. 81'' x 104''.

These printing blocks, made in Lowell, Massachusetts are of the type used by Philena Moxley. The large elephant block was suitable for printing a hooked rug pattern, the smaller pieces for embroidery borders. Elephant, 8'' x 15''. Hands with cards, 8'' x 10''. Three embroidery edgings: 4'' x 2''; 3'' x 1''; 2'' x 1''. (Private Collection)

Philena Moxley

As a young girl, Philena Moxley was employed by Misters Thomas Leland and William Chambers, proprietors of a "fancy goods" shop in the textile manufacturing city of Lowell, Massachusetts. Chambers had traveled to Lowell from England around 1840, bringing with him a collection of stamps used for printing embroidery patterns. The stamps, which Philena used in the shop, were wooden blocks with thin strips of copper and brass hammered into them to form designs. In order to print a pattern, the raised metal strips were coated with a thin paste of flour, water, and powdered blue pigment. By grasping the finger holes drilled on the back, the block was turned upside down and pressed upon a piece of cloth. Once the block was removed, the printed design remained on the fabric.

In 1867, the twenty-three year old Miss Moxley purchased a large number of the embroidery blocks from Leland's brother, William, for the sum of $225. With the stamps in her possession, Philena began her own career as an embroidery stamper. She invested in a prime piece of land and constructed a combination, house and "fancy goods" store. Her shop attracted an impressive clientele and the embroidery stamping business thrived. Philena was soon aware that the blocks could be used to print patterns for her customers that enjoyed hooking rugs. Using large animal designs and others, she stamped burlap hooked rug patterns on demand. Her success warranted the opening of a second shop in the north shore town of Salem. Her sister, Melona, was left in charge of the original shop. Melona, being of frail health and constitution, was unable to manage the store alone and after a successful year in business, Philena closed the Salem shop and returned to Lowell.

Philena married a widower named Jesse Parker in 1880. She raised Jesse's two sons and gave birth to two daughters. In 1889, she closed the store and, with her family and her embroidery printing blocks, moved to the community of Chelmsford. During a coal strike, in attempts to keep the home fires ablaze, many of the wooden blocks were burned. Among those thrown into the fire were the larger stamps that Philena had used to print her hooked rug patterns. In later years, the remaining embroidery blocks traveled with Philena to Wenham, Massachusetts, where she spent her old age in the company of her daughter. She died in 1937 at the age of ninety-four. Her precious embroidery printing blocks were donated to the Wenham Historical Association and are now housed in the Wenham Museum.

Philena Moxley's business of printing hooked rug patterns was conducted on a small scale. Her enterprising venture was overshadowed by the widespread use of pre-stamped rug patterns from E.S. Frost and Company of Biddeford, Maine. Though seemingly insignificant, the story of Philena Moxley is an important one.

A closer look.

Pattern No. 6. This rug maker chose to work Frost's design emphasizing a preference for red and pink flowers. Circa 1880. 36'' x 63''.

Edward Sands Frost

The increased popularity of rug hooking after the Civil War can be attributed to Edward Sands Frost, the first widely known commercial maker of hooked rug patterns. Born on New Year's Day in 1843, Frost led a quiet life in the rural community of Lyman, Maine. When the North and South divided and duty called, he enlisted in Company E of the First Maine Cavalry. Discharged in 1863 due to poor health, Frost returned to Maine and to his awaiting wife, Ellen Whitehouse. He secured a position as machinist for the Saco Water and Power Plant, but illness forced his early retirement.

The following is an excerpt from the 1888 *Biddeford Times*, which describes, in Frost's own words, the story of his success.

Edward Sands Frost 1843-1894

By the advice of my physician, who recommended out-door work, I went into the tin peddling business which I followed till the spring of 1870. During this time, by close economy, I saved my first thousand dollars, and it was the proudest day of my life, when in January, '69, after taking account of stock, I found I had invested in household goods $200.00, in team outfits $175.00, in staple goods and cash in bank $700.00. As the profits did not average over two dollars per day, it had required the strictest economy to support my family and save that amount. It was a hard struggle, but that is the only way a poor man can get capital to go into business with. It is easy enough to make money, if a man has money to work with.

It was during the winter of '68 that my wife, after saving quite a quantity of colored rags that I had collected in my business as a tin peddler, decided to work them into a rug. She went to her cousin, the late Mrs. George Twombley, and had her mark out a pattern, which she did with red chalk on a piece of burlap. After my wife had the pattern properly adjusted to her quilting frame she began to hook the rags with the instrument then used in rug making, which was a hook made of a nail or an old gimlet. After watching her work a while I noticed that she was using a poor hook, so, being a machinist, I went to work and made the crooked hook which was used so many years afterward in the rug business, and is still in vogue today.

While making the hook I would occasionally try it on the rug to see if it was all right as to size, and in this way I got interested in the rug. I had 'caught the fever' as they used to say. So every evening I worked on the rug until it was finished, and it was while thus engaged that I first conceived the idea of working up an article that is to-day about as staple as cotton cloth and sells the world over. Every lady that ever made a rug knows that it is very pleasant and bewitching work on a pretty pattern, but tiresome and hard on plain figure; and so it proved to me. After working four evenings on the rug I told my wife I thought I could make a better design myself than that we were at work on, so after we finished our rug I got a piece of burlap and taking a pencil, I wrote my first design and then put it on to the cloth and worked the flower and scroll already for the ground-work.

We showed it to our neighbors and they were so well pleased with it that I got orders for some twenty or more patterns like it within three days. So you see I got myself into the business right away. I put in my time evenings and stormy days sketching designs, giving only the outlines in black. There was not enough in it to devote my whole time to the business, and as the orders came in faster than I could fill them, I began, Yankee-like, to study some way to do them quicker. Then the first idea of stencilling presented itself to me.

Did I go to Boston to get my stencils made? Oh, no, I went out into my stable where I had some old iron and some old wash boilers I had bought for their copper bottoms, took the tin off them and made my first stencil out of it. Where did I get the tools? Why I found them in the same place, in my stable among the old iron. I got there some old files, half flat and half round, took them to the tin shop of Cummings & West and forged my tools to cut the stencil with. I made a cutting block out of old lead and zinc.

After fitting myself out with tools I began making small stencils of single flowers, scrolls, leaves, buds, etc., each one on a small plate; then I could with a stencil brush print in ink in plain figures faster than I could sketch. Thus I had reduced ten hours' labor to two and a half hours. I then had the art down fine enough to allow me to fill all my orders, so I began to print patterns and put them in my peddler's cart and offer them for sale. The news of my invention of stamped rugs spread like magic and many a time as I drove through the streets of Biddeford and Saco a lady would appear at the door or window, swinging an apron or sun bonnet, and shouting at the top of her voice, say are you the rug man? Do you carry rugs all marked out? I at once became known as Frost, the rug man, and many Biddeford citizens still speak of me in that same way.

My rug business increased and I soon found that I could not print fast enough: I also found it difficult to duplicate my patterns, or make two exactly alike as many of my customers would call for a pattern

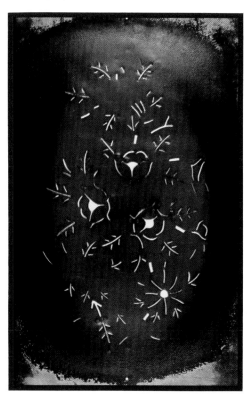

A metal stencil showing the signs of repeated use. (Courtesy of W. Cushing and Company)

just like Mrs. So and so's. Then I began to make a whole design on one plate. At first it seemed impossible, but I was willing to try, so I obtained a sheet of zinc and printed on it and cut out the design. This process I continued to follow till I had some fourteen different designs on hand, ranging from a yard long and a half a yard wide to two yards long and a yard wide. These plates gave only the outline in black and required only one impression to make the pattern complete, yet it was by far the hardest part of the whole affair to make stencils so as to take a good impression, and I think there is not a stencil workman in this country that would consider it possible to cut so large a plate with such fine figures and take an impression from it. It required a great deal of patience, for I was just thirty days cutting the first one when I laid it on the table the center plate would not touch the table by two and a half inches. As the plate of zinc lay smooth before being cut, I knew it must be the cutting that caused the trouble; I studied into the problem and learned that in the cutting the metal expanded, so I expanded the uncut portion in proportion to that which was cut and the plate then lay smooth. This I did with a hammer and it took two days' time.

When the plate was finished I could print with it a pattern in four minutes that had previously required ten hours to sketch by hand. I then thought I had my patterns perfect, so I began to prepare them for the market. I remember well the first trip I made through Maine and part of New Hampshire, trying to sell my goods to the dry goods trade. I failed to find a man who dared invest a dollar in them; in fact, people did not know what they were for, and I had to give up trying for a while and go from house to house. There I found plenty of purchasers, for I found the ladies knew what the patterns were for.

Next I began coloring the patterns by hand, as I had some call for colored goods. The question of how to print them in colors so as to sell them at a profit seemed to be the point on which the success of the business hung, and it took me over three months to settle it. I shall never forget the time and place it came to me, for it had become such a study that I could not sleep nights. It was in March, 1870, one morning about two o'clock. I had been thinking how I could print the bright colors in with the dark ones so as to make clear prints. My mind as so fixed on the problem that I could not sleep, so I turned and twisted and all at once I seemed to hear a voice in my room say: 'Print your bright colors first and then the dark ones.' That settled it, and I was so excited that I could not close my eyes in sleep the rest of the night and I tell you I was glad when morning came so that I could get to town to buy the stock for the plates with which to carry out my idea.

At the end of the week I had one design made and printed in colors. It proved a success. Then I sold my tin peddling business and hired a room in the building on Main Street just above the savings bank, where I began in the month of April, 1870 to print patterns in colors. I did my own work at first for four months and then employed one man. In September I had two men in my employ, and in November I opened a salesroom in Boston through Gibbs and Warren. Then it took four men in December and ten men during the rest of the winter. Many of the business men here will remember what an excitement my business created, for there were very few men who had faith in my bonanza. I remember having seen well known business men stand in the street near Shaw's block and point over at my goods that were hung out and laugh at the idea (as they afterward told me) of my making a living out of such an undertaking. Well, I guess they will admit I did make a living out of it, as I continued to manufacture rug patterns there, all of my own designs, till the fall of '76, when I was so reduced in health that I sold out my business and left Biddeford November 2nd, for Pasadena, California, where I have since made my home.

An antique Frost pattern, No 71. Not all burlap patterns from E.S. Frost and Co. were stenciled with color. (Courtesy of Country Squire Antiques)

Pattern No. 1. A consistent red and green color scheme used throughout this hooked rug accounts for its overall harmony. Dated 1876. 35'' x 68''. (Private Collection)

In 1878, the American Institute Fair of New York awarded Frost a Medal of Excellence; in Boston he received a diploma from the Mechanic Fair.

Frost sold his company to James A. Strout, Mayor of Biddeford, Maine, who continued to do business under the name of E. S. Frost & Company until 1900. During this time, several small companies began to print and distribute rug patterns, many copying from Frost's original compositions, which were never copyrighted. Ebenezer Ross of Toledo, Ohio, invented and sold an "automated" punch hook, with which the rug maker could increase hooking speed and output of rugs. In order to boost sales of his new hook, Ross published in 1891, a catalog of patterns, the majority being variations of Frost's handiwork. Two designs by Ross, though often mistakenly attributed to Frost, are the Mastiff Dog pattern and the popular, Lion and Palm. As the pattern business flourished in the East, Frost had regained his health in the West. He was able to make several trips home to Maine before his death during the spring of 1894.

Many felt that the mass produced patterns stifled creativity; one must realize that Frost's efforts kept women and men hooking at a time when the craft was near extinction. Frost's collection of patterns numbered more than 180, utilizing 750 zinc, copper, and lead hand-cut stencils. These stencils passed through many hands and fortunately were saved from being sold as scrap metal. The Henry Ford Museum in Dearborn, Michigan presently has the original stencils in their collection. Copies of the original Frost patterns are available from W. Cushing and Company in Kennebunkport, Maine. His well-executed designs are easily recognized by experienced collectors of antique hooked rugs. Often seen in shops and at auction, the Frost pattern rugs command respect and high prices.

Pattern No. 36. A King Charles Spaniel is portrayed lying upon a checkerboard floor. Behind him, a flecked background. Circa 1880. 32'' x 43''. (Courtesy of Joan Moshimer) (Photo by Robert Moshimer)

Pattern No. 17. A pair of ducks wait by water's edge. Circa 1880. 16'' x 35''.

A Frost geometric pattern. The checkerboard design was used in many of his animal designs. Note the familiar corner scrolls. 1890-1910. 23'' x 43''. (Courtesy of Wenham Cross Antiques)

Another example of a Frost dog. This pattern offers similar corner scrolls, but places a rose, leaves and buds at each side of the animal. Circa 1880. (Private Collection of Emerson Greenaway) (Photo by Jane Sampson)

For those who tired of hooking smooth curlicue scrolls, Frost offered several patterns with this bold, angular design. Circa 1890. 27" x 43". (Private Collection)

A Frost design combining leaf corners and floral bouquet. Circa 1890. 24" x 39".

Frost used this Maine Scroll to frame many of his compositions. Circa 1890. 30" x 39". (Private Collection)

Pattern No. 79. An ornate oval frame holds a cluster of flowers. Circa 1880. 16'' x 28''. (Private Collection)

The center of this rug was copied from a Frost floral. The borders of hearts, flower buds, and leaves are the rug hooker's original design. Circa 1880. 20'' x 37''. (Private Collection)

Pattern No. 13. A pleasing choice of colors that have become mellow with age. Circa 1870. 25'' x 37''. (Private Collection)

Pattern No. 34. A floral wreath is framed by a crude scroll-like border. Circa 1880. 29'' x 53''.

Pattern No. 89. A lamb rests within a scrolled frame. Circa 1880. 24'' x 39''. (Private Collection)

Pattern No. 42. The rug maker hooked the wicker of the basket to resemble a checkerboard, its handle is partially hidden by blooms and leaves. The corner designs were often used by Frost. Circa 1880. 26'' x 41''. (Private Collection)

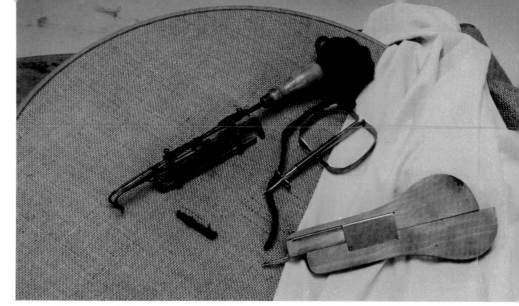

Automatic hooks. The top mechanical hook is much like that which was sold by Ebenezer Ross.

E. Ross & Company, Pattern No. 47. A running riderless horse. Late 19th century. (Collection of Lynn D. Trusdell)

A completed hooked rug from E. Ross & Company's Pattern No. 47. 20th century. (Collection of Lynn D. Trusdell)

The popular Lion and the Palm pattern is often attributed to Frost, though it is believed that Ebenezer Ross is responsible for this design. Ross copied Frost's Lion, reversed his direction, added more foliage, palm trees and an additional lion in the background. Note the long feminine eye lashes on the large male lion. Circa 1900. 32'' x 60''. (From the William Farnsworth Homestead-Farm)

Pictured is a copy of the Frost Lion Pattern No. 176. It features a single male lion and sparse vegetation. (Courtesy of W. Cushing and Company)

Another example of the Ross lion. Late 19th century. (Photo Courtesy of Stephen and Eleanor Score)

Possibly a Ross pattern depicting a dog with fluffy tail. Vegetation is like that of the Ross lion pattern. This pet rests upon a patchwork ground. 1880-1900. 28'' x 54''. (Courtesy of Joan Moshimer) (Photo by Robert Moshimer)

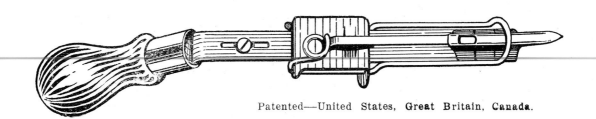

Patented—United States, Great Britain, Canada.

GARRETT'S
"Bluenose" Rug Hooker

Price $1.00

FOR MAKING HOOKED YARN RUGS

Garrett's Bluenose Hooker should not be confused with any other device for making hooked rugs, as it is entirely different, and much superior to anything yet offered for sale. It is a simple little tool with which you can make rugs, and better rugs, very much faster than any other way.

I wish I could step into your home right now, and show you just what this little machine will do, or show you some of the beautiful rugs we are making with the Bluenose Hooker every day. I know you would fall in love with the rugs and appreciate the value of the hooker at once.

If you could see some of the letters we receive from women telling us how pleased they are with Garrett's Bluenose Hooker, you would be convinced immediately. One woman has just recently ordered her fourteenth hooker. She has been making some nice rugs, and naturally is proud of them. She is not our agent, nor selling the hooker for profit, but her enthusiasm and the beauty of her rugs has induced her friends to try it too, hence the fourteen hookers.

The Bluenose Hooker is just about Six Times as Fast as the Ordinary Rug Hook

The "Bunny" rug (No. 7115) has been made in less than five hours with the Bluenose Hooker. We have here a very respectable rug made by a girl seven years old, and a girl of thirteen made a rug (S-42), which won first prize at the Pictou Exhibition. We have made in our own factory over two thousand yarn rugs, some of these 7 x 9 ft.

The Bluenose Hooker is made especially for working with yarn. It will work rags if they are cut fine enough, or if the rag is made of thin material, so that it does not overtax the capacity of the needle. Hosiery cut around and around so as to make a good long rag works beautifully. But the ideal material is yarn. The hooked yarn rug is becoming more and more popular every day. Women are learning to appreciate the advantage of yarn over rags.

Yarn is so Much Easier and Nicer to Work

and your finished rug will be so soft and velvety in texture and so much more satisfactory in every way.

An advertising brochure of the Garrett's "Bluenose" rug hooker and assorted patterns. 1928-1929.

Garrett's "Bluenose"

Garrett's Bluenose hooked rug patterns were printed and distributed from 1892 until 1974. The company was based in Nova Scotia, with distributors in the United States and England. The Bluenose pattern catalog featured hundreds of varying designs which could be hooked with rag or with the yarns they dyed and sold. At the height of prosperity, their mailing list contained the names of 20,000 women. Pictured are a small sample of their designs.

Many Canadian made rug patterns featured maple leaves in their designs. Circa 1940.

Pattern No. 193 is made in three sizes, namely,—2¼ yd., 2 yd. and 1¾ yd. size. (For prices see list page 6).

Rug Hooks 25c. each
(We Pay Postage)

Pattern No. 283, made in four sizes, namely,—1¾ yd. size, 1½ yd., 1¼ yd., 1 yd. and 32 in. size. (See price list page 6).

Ask your dealer for BLUENOSE materials for making Hooked Rugs.

Pattern No. S-721, size 1¼ yd. x 28 ins. (Made in this size only).

Price each $1.00

Hooked from Garrett's pattern No. S-721, featured in the 1928-1929 brochure.

A silhouette of a moose against a Northern landscape. Circa 1950. (Courtesy of Robert E. Richards Antiques)

Corners of stars and moon add a note of whimsy to this collage of shapes and designs. Circa 1930. (From the Collection of Sweet Nellie)

Good luck runs out of this rug whose background is hooked of hemp twine. 30'' x 63''. (Private Collection)

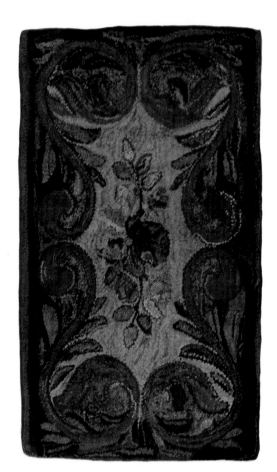

Large curlicue scrolls frame a simple spray of flowers. 29'' x 52''. (Private Collection of S.H. Kearney)

A Hooked Rug is a Joy Forever
They are Easy to Make and Not Expensive

Mr. Ralph W. Burnham admires a finely hooked rug. (Courtesy of Annie A. Spring)

Annie A. Spring, niece of the late Ralph Burnham, kindly allowed me the use of her uncle's collection of photographs and Trading Post memorabilia. For this privilege, I am very thankful. As a young girl, Annie worked in the rug sales room and was often called upon by her uncle to demonstrate for interested customers, the ease of rug hooking. Seated at a rug frame, she hooked the strips of rag, providing testimony to the fact that even a child could master the craft. Today Annie is a talented rug hooking teacher. Though busy with many classes, she finds time to write articles about Mr. Burnham, and continues as her uncle did, to enthusiastically promote the joy of hooked rugs.

The House of Burnham

The soul of the apartment, is in the carpet; from it
are deduced not only the hues but the form of all the
objects incumbent.

Edgar Allan Poe

Ralph W. Burnham was an antique dealer
well-known for his fine selection of furniture
and an overwhelming collection of hooked rugs.
His Antique Trading Post located in the sea
coast town of Ipswich, Massachusetts, attracted
an impressive chauffeur-driven clientele. The
long list of notable customers included the du
Ponts of Winterthur in Delaware, interior
designer Henry Sleeper, popular 1920s actor
John Mack Brown, and department stores such
as John Wanamaker, Marshall Fields, and B.
Altman Company.

During the turn of the century, Mr. Burnham
and his crew of "pickers" scoured the New
England countryside in search of heirlooms
from days gone by. What Burnham found in
many of the homes he visited were caches of
hooked rugs; hand crafted treasures of all ages,
sizes and colors, some in pristine condition,
others in various stages of disrepair. Realizing
that colorful handmade floor coverings would
enhance old furnishings and aware that uniquely
designed textiles would attract interior
decorators, Burnham bought all the hooked
pieces he and his workers could find, regardless
of condition.

By 1905, Burnham advertised an inventory of
over 3,000 and was appropriately dubbed "The
Hooked Rug Magnate". All cleaning and
restoration work, including outside customer

Burnham admired the design of this rug and offered the
pattern in his catalog. Origins unknown. Circa 1890. 30''
x 46''.

HOOKED RUG REPAIRING AT BURNHAM'S, IPSWICH

HOOKED RUGS *and* BRAIDED RUGS

I have been making and repairing these rugs since 1905.

At my works in Ipswich I employ the only real corps of experts in the world. The big rug dealers of America know this and take advantage of it. So should you.

3000 *Hooked Rugs* now assembled here offer a wide variety for you to choose from.

BURNHAM'S HOOKED RUG BOOK, mailed for only 25c in stamps, has 44 pages. It is chock full of information on this interesting craft. It tells you "How to Make Hooked Rugs," carefully leading you, step by step, so that even a child may learn. It shows fifty designs in illustrations. It tells the size, the price and the amount of material required to make up each design and it tells the history of Hooked Rugs. This useful book shows the frames, the set up, the hooks and the complete kit with which these fine rugs can be fashioned.

For

Hooked Rugs   Braided Rugs   Rug Repairs

Patterns and Supplies

BURNHAM'S IS THE PLACE

Repair room. (Courtesy of Annie A. Spring)

requests passed through the repair shop on the second floor. Six to twenty women were kept busy six days a week from 8 am to 5 pm. For those clients with special needs, the repair room staff made custom designed rugs and hooked to order oversized reproductions of antique rugs. Burnham was no stranger to the tools of his trade and often assisted the ladies upstairs with their projects.

To preserve the antique rug designs that he fancied, Burnham made paper tracings of many of the rugs that passed through the shop. In 1922 he started producing burlap rug patterns for sale. His mail order catalogs featuring copies of the old hooked rugs brought in orders from all over the United States and Canada.

The economic problems that blanketed the country during the 1930s took its toll on the antique market. Sales of furniture and hooked rugs dropped, but requests for patterns increased considerably. During these lean years, Burnham assisted hooked rug authority, W.W. Kent with the writing of his first book. Many of the rugs pictured in Kent's trilogy are from the House of Burnham collection.

Ralph Burnham died in 1938. A love for hooking and his efforts to restore thousands of damaged pieces have given today's generation the opportunity to view many antique hooked rugs that would have been lost if not for his expertise. Burnham's widow, Nellie, continued the pattern business until 1957. Eventually it was sold to Ruth Hall, a talented rug hooking teacher and pattern designer from New Hampshire. Mrs. Hall in turn passed the designs on to W. Cushing and Company of Kennebunkport, Maine which now reprints many of the Burnham favorites.

Arthur Warren Johnson, in the 1930s wrote an eloquent piece, "An Adventure in Contentment", which Mr. Burnham published and distributed. It read as follows:

Early this winter I sat reading in my home. The book was interesting enough yet I was seized by a feeling of irritation at all about me. The electric refrigerator hummed in the distance, the low growl of the motor of the automatic heat cut into the air, the harsh clang of the telephone had interrupted me several times and outside the occasional starting of a car or the grinding of brakes added confusion of noise.

Expertly designed and hooked rug of flowers and scrolls, one of the many offered by Mr. Burnham. (Courtesy of Annie A. Spring)

Advertisement with photo of women hooking a large rug.
(Courtesy of Annie A. Spring)

Confessing the creature comfort of all these things yet I was irritated knowing that the price paid was that of a constant nervous irritation. Weary of my home with all its mechanical noises I went out for a walk to obtain quiet and some soothing sur-surcease from these demands made on one's nerves by a mechanical age. Outside, living was a little better. Cars rushed past me with subdued roar, and a tractor hopped noisily along the hard pavement.

Walking with no other motive than to get outside the town with its confusion of noises, I was suddenly aware that I was opposite Mr. Burnham's Antique Trading Post. Pausing in a moment's indecision, I could not resist the invitation of the memorials of another age spread before me in the quaint windows. They all spoke the language of a quiet, peaceful past, and so I entered.

One does not have to be an invited guest to enter Mr. Burnham's Trading Post for it is its own welcome. No professional clerks sallied up to me to oppress me with high-powered salesmanship and make me ill at ease. Mr. Burnham, busy as usual just sang out, "Make yourself at home; the place is yours while you are here." And he spoke truth, for indeed when one is in this sanctuary of the past, one enters into it as a heritage and no guide is needed other than fancy.

It is pleasant indeed to step back into another age, as if a clock slipped back three cogs and each cog a century, and to live the remembrance of thing past. Within the House of Burnham the past seems to live in its fullest in the "Home of the Rug," as that section of Mr. Burnham's retreat might be called. Here is industry without noise, save the occasional laughter of happy workers or the faint soft calls of the famous Burnham goats coming in from out in the fields.

Within this place I sat down comfortably on a great pile of hooked rugs, for they were soft to look at and inviting. Of course this was something one would never think of doing in the rug department of any city store. In such a place the human relationship is entirely different. One must stand at attention, tense, ill at ease in a commercial relationship. None of this in the House of Burnham. Of course the rugs were for sale; one took that for granted without bothering about it over much, for the spirit of the commercialism has not corroded essential New Englandism. It was, indeed, a Trading Post, but there is a world of difference between its methods and that of a commercial sales establishment. In the Trading Post one waits on fancy, one has time to let beauty take one captive. There is none of that unpleasant feeling which one experiences in a house of commerce where, continually at one's elbow, buzzing like a mosquito, is a salesperson forcing decisions on you against your will, that he may crowd as many sales into as little time as possible.

And so it was that I sat taking my ease letting fancy master the long moment, for here about me was the past recaptured. Before me was living fold-art, one of the few America has produced and one which the poets of commerce, like Mr. Burnham, have kept alive in the face of the gnawing competition of the machine.

There, fancy free, on that pile of soft rugs glowing with colors I thought, soberly, that without doubt the machine could produce very efficient floor coverings; but, I asked myself, does one want more than efficiency in those things which are one's constant companions, those things which should be things of beauty? The answer was a decided "Yes!"

The home is the one place where the individual can express his personality, where one extends one's personality into the things about him. That which the machine produces expresses nothing but deadly routine and sameness of the machine. The spirit of man has and does demand more than this.

In a peculiar sense the hooked rug is the expression of the spirit of America. The perfumed mystic East ... Persia, Iran, Syria, Agra ... Has always chosen the rug as a means to express its essence of race and culture. Some of these rugs have been an entire lifetime in their making. Here in other days in New England the same medium was chosen to express a consciousness of America. Patterns of ships and native flowers, the rose and the lilac, all tell of these things. These ancient patterns have their roots in our own soil, but they are touched and illumined with fancy and imagination. No two are alike and each has its own claim to being, for it expresses a human personality.

Beyond the patterns are the colors and they, too, speak their language and it is the language of music, for color blends with color, in harmony and counterpoint and many a sweet melody.

Fancy free was not content to stop here and it carried me into a full realization of the pressure of our present American living and I realized that our active fingers, hands and minds must needs have something akin to the relaxation of music, some way of escape from the tenseness of each day. Music as an escape from the pressure of living is ideal; yes, but how many of us have been given either the ability or means to do this?

The fashioning, the creating of a hooked rug does exactly for the individual that which music does and to me they seem very closely related.

Diamond shapes for a background surround simple flowers and leaves hooked in a center rectangle. Part of the Burnham Collection. (Courtesy of Annie A. Spring)

Unusual inner circle small scroll wreath and two stars are found on this hooked rug from the House of Burnham Collection. (Courtesy of Annie A. Spring)

97

Burnham's Antiques

| Vol. III. | IPSWICH, MASS., JANUARY 1, 1927. | No. 1. |

Burnham's Antique Trading Post, Old Bay Road, Ipswich, Massachusetts
Headquarters of the Hooked Rug Industry in America

Cover of *Burnham's Antiques*. (Courtesy of Annie A. Spring)

I watched the workers as their fingers sped through the heaps of gay colors transmuting them into form and design and I knew then that creation, either of a drama, a poem, a great commercial enterprise, or a hooked rug, was a sure way to happiness. I knew, also, that here was something American living needed; a simple, pleasant and creative way of escape from the deadly routine of bread and butter.

I picked up one of the hooks and some of the bright colored material and sat down at a vacant frame and played with these things. Soon I was fascinated with the movements my fingers were making, the birth of a pattern of color on the soft burlap background, and then all the tenseness of the afternoon dissolved and for the moment I became one of the lords of this earth, a creator, for under my fingers was growing something from inside me into outer expression.

I knew my feelings were the same the artist feels when he puts his brush to canvas, for was not this burlap a form of canvas, and was not this hook as capable of a deft motion as any brush? Yes, I too was painting on canvas with hook and colour my dream pattern of colour and form as much as any artist in his studio.

The old Greeks had a notion that the function of any art was the cleansing, or purging, of human living of its dross. There is much truth in this, and the fashioning of a rug does this very thing. As one works all the cares away, one becomes lost in the mystery of color and form and a pleasant relaxation of creative activity takes the place of stress and tenseness.

Not all medicines come in a bottle and I am convinced that Mr. Burnham in preserving this heritage of the past is giving to the American people

Page 10 Plate V. *Burnham's Antiques.* (Courtesy of Annie A. Spring)

Price list from *Burnham's Antiques,* January 1, 1927. (Courtesy of Annie A. Spring)

a form of healing they need very much, a form of healing many a nerve specialist would give much to be able to impart to his patients.

And so I sat for a long space and when I left with reluctance I knew I had been in contact with something vital to American living. I knew that Mr. Burnham in his faith in his desire of the American people to create themselves and not be tied in all things to the products of the machine; in these things I knew he was making large and liberal contribution to this thing termed Americanism.

Americanism had its beginnings and its foundations not only in those things which the Founding Fathers accomplished in the realm of politics, but also in what the Founding Mother did within the American home. The preservation of this dual heritage requires devotion not only to the political ideals but also to those things which made the early American woman the sane and wholesome people that they were.

In the loom and the spinning wheel, the hooking and weaving of rugs, these women who were co-founders of our country found poise and balance. For those who come after, it would seem eminently wise that they also walk in the footsteps prepared for them.

Those who know Mr. Burnham know that he is the essence of this older New England. In the age of the machine he has kept the faith of other days. As they were pioneers, so also he is and has been a pioneer. The revival and preservation of this great American folk-art owes much to his vision; and I, humble observer, feel in all sincerity that he contributes as much to American living as many a politician under gilded domes, for his is the Faith of the fathers, that faith which says, "Man liveth not by bread alone."

Popular radiating star makes for a handsome rug at Burnham's Trading Post. (Courtesy of Annie A. Spring)

An impressive rug from the Burnham Collection. (Courtesy of Annie A. Spring)

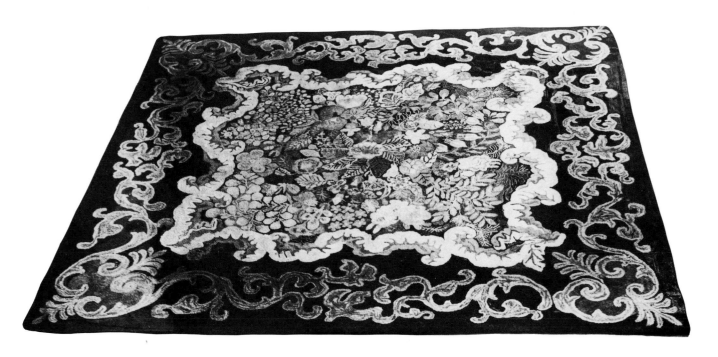

HOOKED RUGS

Welcome rug pictured in this ad was hooked from a Frost
pattern, as were many of the rugs that passed through the
Trading Post. (Courtesy of Annie A. Spring)

The interior of the South Gallery. Beauport-Sleeper, McCann House. (Property of the S.P.N.E.A.)

A hooked rug of sunburst design rests upon the South Gallery floor. Beauport-Sleeper, McCann House. (Property of the S.P.N.E.A.)

Beauport Museum

Beauport, the retreat of Henry Davis Sleeper, (1878-1934), began as a summer cottage and grew into a labyrinth of forty rooms. Each unique space was meticulously planned to showcase the variety of antiques collected by Sleeper, a well-liked, well-to-do Boston bachelor who designed and decorated interiors for such clients as the du Ponts and the Vanderbilts. Located in Massachusetts, along the shore of Gloucester Harbor, Sleeper began construction of Beauport in 1907. In the twenty-seven years that followed, he added room after room to house his increasingly large and varied collection of acquisitions. Sleeper invited his many well known friends and associates to view his treasures, leading his guests through a maze of connecting chambers. Visitors to Beauport would be drawn from a silent and dark paneled room, then suddenly plunged into a space filled with sunlight and echoes of the sounds of the sea and crashing surf. Period furnishings and decorative objects crammed every corner.

After his death in 1934, the house and its contents were purchased by the McCann family, of F.W. Woolworth fame. Though pursued by collectors and museums to relinquish parts of the collection or to sell the contents of certain rooms, the McCann children, following the wishes of their deceased parents, presented Beauport in its entirety to The Society for the Preservation of New England Antiquities. Today, The Beauport-Sleeper, McCann House is open to the public from May through October. A large collection of fine hooked rugs, many purchased from antiques and hooked rug dealer, Ralph Burnham, remain and function in the extraordinary summer home of Henry Sleeper.

Strawberry Hill Room. Beauport-Sleeper, McCann House. (Property of the Society for the Preservation of New England Antiquities)

An attractive corner of the Strawberry Hill Room. Beauport-Sleeper, McCann House. (Property of the Society for the Preservation of New England Antiquities)

A view of the Belfry Room. Beauport-Sleeper, McCann House. (Property of the S.P.N.E.A.)

Light streams through the Indian Room porch windows upon a simple geometric rug. Beauport-Sleeper, McCann House. (Property of the S.P.N.E.A.)

In one of Beauport's many halls hangs the Wedding Rug. As the ceremony commenced, the couple stood together upon this floral rug. The two center flowers represent the bride and groom. (Property of S.P.N.E.A.)

The pattern of painted roses that grace the chair backs is repeated in the center of this large hooked rug. Beauport-Sleeper, McCann House. (Property of the S.P.N.E.A.)

The North Wind blows down upon the island of Newfoundland and the partial coastline of Labrador. The small scattered houses represent the early hospital stations. St. Anthony, home of Dr. Grenfell, the hospital sight and the headquarters of the Grenfell Industrial Department, is pictured directly across from the spouting whale. The areas of land were hooked from unraveled strips of burlap, sea and figures worked from strips of rayon and silk jersey. 31'' x 41''.

Grenfell Labrador Industries

Blessed are the toilers who serve mankind by their labor. But blessed above all are they whose hands bring forth beauty from the common things that we pass by.

Robert Weston

During the summer of 1892, a small ship carrying medical supplies reached the shore of Newfoundland. The seventeen-day passage from England had been complicated by rough seas, icebergs, and heavy fog. The crew of three was now confronted by the smoldering remains of St. John's. For the third time in its history, Newfoundland's capital city had been destroyed by fire. From the ship's deck, the young, energetic English doctor, Wilfred Grenfell, watched as thousands fled their burned out homes. "Go North," he was advised. "Follow the men that fish the Labrador Coast; the need there is greater than ours." This unselfish attitude in the face of their own disaster greatly and forever impressed Grenfell. The mates hauled anchor and sailed into the frigid Atlantic, bound for Labrador.

The most wretched of living conditions were found along the desolate coast. Remote fishing villages consisted of poorly constructed huts scattered haphazardly on the rocky cliffs. Many families were in dire need of food, clothing, and medical treatment. Daily life was a struggle, worsened for many months by nature's full fury of ice and snow. The Northern people were proud and hard working; faced with unending hardships, they remained optimistic.

For the next forty years, Dr. Grenfell sailed the Labrador and Newfoundland Coasts setting up medical stations and maintaining them. When frozen waters blocked a ship's passing, he would travel the snow covered miles by dogsled. With no money and not willing to accept charity, the fishermen would pay for the doctor's services by any means they could. A broken leg would be set in exchange for firewood, fresh game, or a hand made trinket.

Periodically, Grenfell would leave the North and travel to England and the United States to lecture, raise funds, and gather clothing donations. His vibrant and congenial personality attracted many skilled professionals and volunteers who gladly journeyed North to help the Grenfell Mission with their medical, educational, and social improvement projects.

Sir Wilfred Grenfell on board his Hospital Ship in Labrador. (Courtesy of the Sir Wilfred Thomason Grenfell Historical Society)

A mat maker's frame rests atop an old stenciled pattern. The printed burlap was carefully laced onto the frame creating a very taut surface to hook upon. Fine strips of silk and rayon jersey cut from hosiery, such as pictured, were used to hook the designs. The mat frame, a gift to the author, was made by Max Colbourne, who worked directly with Dr. Grenfell and the Grenfell Mission for over 50 years. (Pattern Courtesy of the Grenfell Handicrafts)

A dog team, komatik, and two men pause to check their load. Dr. Grenfell encouraged visiting artists to submit drawings for the mat makers to copy. It is believed that painter Steve Hamilton is responsible for this design. An experienced mat maker would be employed to hook a pattern of great detail, such as this one pictured. 34" x 46". (Courtesy of the Grenfell House Museum)

A close up reveals the fine quality of this mat maker's work.

Mat hooking was a native industry, generations old, when Grenfell arrived in Newfoundland and Labrador. The mats provided a warm and colorful floor covering for the modest homes. By kerosene lamp, the long winters were passed seated with perfect posture at a simple, four sided wooden frame. With a bent nail for a hook, an old grain sack, and worn materials, the abstract designs came to life. The cloth was carefully cut into the longest strip possible of ¼" width or less. The hooking was done in straight, horizontal lines, tightly packed with as many as 200 loops per square inch. Dr. Grenfell described these early rugs as "ugly", but noted that the craftmanship was of the highest quality. With improvements in color and design, he felt the mats could be sold abroad and be a source of income for the women.

The Industrial Department located in St. Anthony, the northern most tip of Newfoundland, was formed by the Grenfell Mission to create work for the people along the coast. By providing quality materials to work with, making constructive suggestions and improvements, the local crafts could be transformed into a saleable product. Dr. Grenfell, his wife, Anne, and numerous volunteer craftspeople, succeeded in this undertaking. Word quickly spread that handicrafts such as carving, weaving, and mat hooking could be traded at the Industrial Department for clothing bundles, food vouchers, or cash. The work rooms of the small building were soon overflowing with the crafts awaiting shipment to the United States. The Mission's record book listed close to 2,000 handicraft workers, the majority being women mat makers. With this many hands hooking, the mat department became the busiest and most profitable in the Industrial.

As the demand for the mats grew, it became apparent that the mission would need more materials to hook with. During a lecture tour in the United States, the ingenious Doctor appealed to the ladies in the audience to donate their discarded silk and rayon stockings to his cause. His campaign, heralded by the slogan, "When your stocking begins to run, let it run to Labrador", was a tremendous success. The hose of the affluent American socialites made their way North by the ship load. The light colored silk and rayon jersey from stockings, night gowns, and under garments, could be easily dyed and made a superior hooking medium.

Though heavily involved with hospital affairs, Dr. Grenfell found time to sketch new mat designs. His Northern themes of polar bears basking on icebergs, dog teams racing, and geese flying became popular mat subjects. He also persuaded artists visiting Newfoundland and Labrador to submit landscapes for the ladies to copy and hook on burlap. Improvements in color were made by dyeing the stockings to pleasing pastel shades. With the support of creative minds, the scenes on the mats took on perspective and depth. The finished products were exquisite works of art sought after by the buying public overseas.

During these prosperous days, the mat industry was run with assembly line precision. Each woman working in the Industrial building was given a specific job essential for the efficient and proper mat production. The work rooms bustled with activity. Makeshift stoves kept the dye pots boiling. Wooden racks, ordinarily used for drying salted cod fish, bowed under the weight of the wet, colored hosiery. The cutting of the thousands of dyed stockings was a process similar to peeling an apple. Starting at the top of the stocking, the woman would carefully snip the jersey, spiraling down to the tip of the toe. The unbroken length, ⅛" wide, was pulled and stretched and rolled in a ball to be kept for later use. Very finely woven burlap, or brin as it was called, purchased by the Mission in commercial-size bolts, was cut and printed by hand with the Northern scenes. For lack of a better material, discarded x-ray film from the medical stations was cut into a master stencil. The stiff, plastic-like film adapted well to the ink printing and could be used over and over. Small swatches of the dyed fabric were pinned to the appropriate areas of the pattern. The fool-proof kits of stenciled burlap and corresponding colored jersey were distributed among the numerous mat makers to take home and hook in their spare time. Each worker's name and materials received, were recorded in the Industrial Department's ledger.

Men would gladly haul their wives by dogsled or row their dories to St. Anthony for Mat Day. On Friday of each week, the waiting room of the Industrial was filled to capacity with women and their prized bundles. When the crowd began to spill out the doorways, Thursday, in addition to Friday, was reserved for the viewing of the mats. One by one, each woman relinquished her mats to a Grenfell staff member. In exchange for her handiwork, every mat maker walked out of the Industrial's doors with a small amount of money, clothing, or a food voucher, and tucked securely under her arm, more patterns to hook. Mats of inferior quality were always accepted by the staff, but never shipped out of the country.

Those unable to attend Mat Day due to distance or illness sent their finished mats by any means that could be arranged. The slow-moving mail boats and the hospital ships carried the mats up and down the coasts. It was not unusual to see a Labrador steamer struggling through thick ice to reach port, her hole full of cod and her decks adorned with twenty or thirty hooked mats.

Each mat was tagged (when tags were available) with a small, cloth "Grenfell Industries" label and packed for the ocean voyage to the States. The International Grenfell Society successfully operated handicraft shops in Philadelphia and on the prestigious Madison Avenue in New York City. The followers of the recently knighted Sir Wilfred, and Lady Anne Grenfell, frequented these stores, coordinating visits with the arrival of goods and news from the North. Representatives traveled throughout the New England area and as far south as Florida, setting up craft displays for interested groups. The Great Depression of 1929 found Grenfell working twice as hard for half the funding, but determined as ever. Despite a second heart attack, the doctor and his small army of volunteers managed to keep the interest in the Northern people and their crafts alive well into the 1930s.

In 1939, Grenfell made a final trip along his beloved coast of Labrador. After seeing the many friends and associates he had gathered during his forty years of service, Grenfell quietly retired to a Vermont home. Death overcame him in October, 1940. His ashes were sent to St. Anthony to rest beside those of his wife, Anne.

The outbreak of World War II brought a shortage of materials and a general lack of interest in the cottage industry of mat hooking. Women found employment elsewhere and only a few elders continued to hook mats for their own use.

Portrait of a faithful sled dog. Background is hooked to resemble a stained glass window. 11" x 12". (Courtesy of Barbara and Robert Meltzer) (Photo by Stacey Meltzer)

Hunter and his dog chase an unknown prey. 11" x 15". (Courtesy of Barbara and Robert Meltzer) (Photo by Stacey Meltzer)

The Northern Lights illuminate the sky as a dog team, komatik, and men race by. 15'' x 49''. (Collection of Barbara and Robert Meltzer) (Photo by Stacey Meltzer)

A detailed portrait of a leaping trout is placed upon a background of abstract water. 21'' x 26''. (Courtesy of the Grenfell House Museum)

Pictured is a view of St. Anthony Harbor. Two goats and a lone cow graze by the church and in the distance a lighthouse guides dories safely into port. 26'' x 39''. (Collection of Barbara and Robert Meltzer) (Photo by Stacey Meltzer))

Bands of color create a backdrop for this sailing ship. The water reflects the striped sky. 8'' x 9''. (Private Collection)

A fleet of sailing ships, each with a different color deck and one flying a red flag, form a line as they sail into the horizon. This mat was used as a chair cushion. 19'' x 19''. (Collection of Barbara and Robert Meltzer) (Photo by Stacey Meltzer)

This mat of poor condition was hooked entirely from dyed and unraveled pieces of burlap. When materials to hook with ran short, mat makers made do with what was available. 20'' x 32''.

A sail boat navigates past floating ice on its way to the open sea. 27'' x 39''. (Collection of Cindy and Paul Kaplan)

A schooner under full sail passes by a lighthouse displaying a Red Cross flag, indication of a nearby medical station. 25'' x 39''. (Collection of Barbara and Robert Meltzer) (Photo by Stacey Meltzer)

A silhouette of two sail boats. 13'' x 18''. (Courtesy of the Grenfell House Museum)

This sail boat travels on calm waters. 10'' x 14''. (Courtesy of Lynne Weaver Antiques)

Two polar bears meet. The pair of parallel lines crossing the sky are probably power cables; their presence in this scene was of importance to the mat maker. Electricity may have just been brought in to her remote community. 17'' x 19''. (Collection of Barbara and Robert Meltzer) (Photo by Stacey Meltzer)

Sea gulls fly overhead as a polar bear drifts past atop a floating ice pan. The maker hooked the bear's coat from woolen yarn, pulling the loops up higher than the background. She then clipped the wool and went over the hooked fur with a wire brush to make it appear thick and fluffy. 7'' x 10''.

A polar bear peers over the edge of an ice pan. 26'' x 39''. (Collection of Barbara and Robert Meltzer) (Photo by Stacy Meltzer)

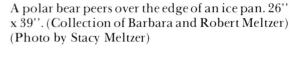

A polar bear gazes across the open sea. Diameter 12''.

Hooked mats were not only made to function as wall hangings and floor rugs, but were used to make decorative pillows, book covers and ladies' pocketbooks. Pictured is a shoulder bag made by stitching two mats together and adding a lining and strap. This scene shows two darker than normal polar bears watching a setting sun. 10'' x 12''. (Collection of Barbara and Robert Meltzer) (Photo by Stacey Meltzer)

Two walruses bask in the day's remaining sunlight. 26'' x 38''. (Collection of Barbara and Robert Meltzer) (Photo by Stacey Meltzer)

A pair of spouting whales perform for an audience of a walrus and swooping gull. (Photo Courtesy of Stephen and Eleanor Score)

A colorful Northern collage. 20" x 27". (Collection of Barbara and Robert Meltzer) (Photo by Stacey Meltzer)

In a letter dated April 29, 1937, Sir Wilfred emphasizes his respect for the Northern people. (Private Collection)

SIR WILFRED GRENFELL, K.C.M.G., M.D.
156 FIFTH AVENUE
NEW YORK, N.Y.

April 29, 1937

Miss E. C. Pierce
Watertown, Mass.

Dear Miss Pierce:

News has just come to Lady Grenfell and me that this coming summer the Clarke Steamship Company is to have the additional service of the beautiful cruising ship the "NORTH STAR".

This is good news indeed not only for our people in the North to whom these cruises mean so much, but for the fortunate passengers who will now have two splendid boats, the "NORTH STAR" and the "NEW NORTHLAND", on which they can take this summer cruise.

Biased as I naturally am, I still feel with all my heart that it would be hard to find a pleasanter, more interesting and more refreshing voyage than the one which this company offers and I can only say that I personally and also on behalf of our Staff and our Northern fishermen, wish them every possible success.

The period of transition between isolation and contact with civilization is always difficult for people in remote parts of the world and it makes a great difference to them as well as to those who are doing their utmost to induce a better life among them, what type of people from "civilization" are presented to them. In this respect they are fortunate in my opinion to have had the passengers from these cruises who always without exception have been a fine type of idealistic people eager to help our splendid Northern fisher folk and not to bring to them those aspects of civilization which are deleterious, nor to pauperize them nor to undermine their self-respect.

We know that many of our friends have wished to visit us in past years but were, perhaps, unable to obtain accomodation on the Clarke steamers, whose popularity has created a demand exceeding their capacity; now, with this new liner, this difficulty will be to a large extent overcome--so let this be "Labrador Year" for you; a hearty welcome awaits you--COME NORTH!

Faithfully yours,

Sir Wilfred Grenfell attending patients aboard the hospital ship, *Stathcona*. (Courtesy of the Grenfell House Museum)

INTERNATIONAL GRENFELL ASSOCIATION

INDUSTRIAL DEPARTMENT

HANDICRAFTS

MADE IN

NORTHERN NEWFOUNDLAND

AND LABRADOR

The Industrial Department of the IGA provides work for convalescent and disabled persons in the Industrial building and gives part time work to many people in their own homes in the production centres and smaller communities. All the work produced is prepared and supervised by the Industrial Department. Ivory, wood and weaving are taught at St. Anthony and hooking, weaving, knitting and sewing sent into the homes. The production centres in Labrador at Cartwright and North West River specialize in fine silk embroidery on Grenfell Cloth, duffle and blanket and do skin and grass work. Harrington Harbour does mostly hooking with some knitting. Our goods are on sale in our own shops at St. Anthony, Cartwright, North West River and Harrington Harbour, at the Grenfell Labrador Medical Mission offices, 48 Sparks Street, Ottawa, or can be obtained through any one of our many agents throughout Canada to whom we sell direct. Any profits realized from this work are used by the Mission for their charitable medical work and for the expansion of the Industrial Department.

IVORY. Walrus tusk, walrus and whale tooth ivory is carved by hand by rasp and file and made into beautiful ashtrays, pins, ear-rings, model animals and figures, paper cutters, etc.

WOOD. Brooches, paper knives, door knockers, book ends, etc., are carved, painted and stained in Northern animal designs, and komatic cribbage boards.

WEAVING. Guest towels, tray cloths, bags and scarves in an assortment of designs and colours, the most outstanding being the embroidered weave designs of dogs, schooners and dogteams and the Northern Lights shading in scarves.

Hooked figures of Inuit children at play are placed upon a background of orange colored burlap. This wall hanging was made in the 1960s. 15" x 30".

HOOKING. Old silk stockings and rayon underwear, collected and sent to us by friends, are bleached and dyed and used in the hooking of picture mats, bags and purses in Northern designs. Floor mats are made of stocking tops, new flannelette or jute.

GRENFELL CLOTH. The washable, wind and shower proof material, made and woven in England to Sir Wilfrid Grenfell's specifications in a wide range of colours is used for the true Northern "Dickie" embroidered and fur trimmed; parka coats, jackets, mittens, slippers, tea cloths and a wide variety of small items such as needle books, coin purses, buttons, bib and place mat sets, belts, etc., all embroidered with Northern designs of dogs, eskimo figures, dogteam, igloo and floral patterns.

DUFFLE & BLANKET. Duffle, the heavy felt-like white blanket material used in the north for vamps, mittens and dickies is made into attractively embroidered garments, slippers and even bedside rugs. Blanket coats, snowsuits, children's coat and hood sets, baby jackets, blankets and sleeping bags—all embroidered.

GRASS WORK. Waste baskets, work baskets, trays and hot plate mat sets of sweet native grass with raffia for color.

SKIN WORK. Sealskin—bark tanned slippers and boots as worn "on coast"—hairseal slippers, white or smoked deerskin slippers, gauntlets, baby mocassins, coin purses and ladies and men's coats—embroidered, beaded, furred.

KNITTING. Mittens, gloves and socks in patterns—all sizes.

An old pamphlet describing the crafts available from the International Grenfell Association.

A night scene of a hunter and his dog as they head for their cabin on the hill. 27'' x 39''.

Grouping gulls are set against a summer landscape. 22'' x 28''. (Collection of Barbara and Robert Meltzer) (Photo by Stacey Meltzer)

A night scene of deer coming to the edge of the woods. Note the slight wisp of a moon and the illuminated cabin windows. 27'' x 41''. (Collection of Barbara and Robert Meltzer) (Photo by Stacey Meltzer)

Canadian geese fly across a color filled sky. 13" x 47". (Collection of Barbara and Robert Meltzer) (Photo by Stacey Meltzer)

A hunter and his dog head for their cabin as darkness draws near. 26" x 40". (Collection of Barbara and Robert Meltzer) (Photo by Stacey Meltzer)

A lone Canadian goose flies above the tree tops. 7" x 9".

Some mats were hooked depicting indigenous plants and flowers. The women mat makers found the designs a pleasant change from scenes of ice and snow. Buyers in the United States with no interest in Northern themes were attracted to the floral patterns of the small table top mats.

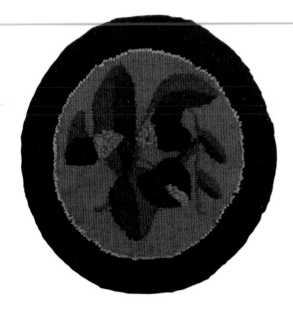

A starfish is hooked behind a land growing flower. Diameter 15''.

Diameter 9''.

Diameter 10''.

8'' x 8''.

Pictured are a sampling of the various Grenfell Industries labels that were sewn on the backs of the finished hooked mats. There are no records to indicate which years certain labels were used, and some mats did leave the St. Anthony headquarters without a cloth tag. In the years before the Grenfell mats became popular collector's items, some antique dealers of questionable reputation, feeling that handicrafts from the North were of little value, removed the labels and tried to convince prospective buyers that the mats were hooked in Maine.

Old Grenfell mat with lone driver and his dog team travel across the snow covered field. (Collection of Barbara and Robert Meltzer) (Photo by Stacey Meltzer)

Northern Lights are the backdrop for a medical team and racing dogs. 1990. 26" x 39". (Private Collection)

Grenfell Handicrafts

The Grenfell Handicrafts label used today.

The Grenfell Handicrafts, reestablished in 1984 and located in St. Anthony, Newfoundland, has a shop filled with hand-embroidered and hand-sewn parkas of Grenfell cloth, sweaters, and many other Northern crafts of quality. Newly hooked mats, whose patterns are traced from old stencils, are available. The designs are protected by International Copyright law and therefore the unhooked patterns are not available to the public. Dr. Grenfell's original intent was that the Northern designs benefit the peoples of Newfoundland and Labrador. His wish will continue to be honored.

Silk stockings are no longer used to hook the mats. The Grenfell Handicraft uses fine wool yarns, the texture of the new mats is similar to that of needlepoint. And as was done in the past, each and every hole of the made to order, tightly woven burlap, is hooked through.

A dog team and two followers dressed in parkas emerge from the woods. 1989. 16" x 24". (Private Collection)

Three dogs pull the medical supply komatik under a cloudless night sky. 1990. 17" x 29". (Private Collection)

Grenfell House Museum, St. Anthony, Newfoundland.

Mat makers hook together on the porch of the Grenfell House Museum, St. Anthony, Newfoundland. Summer 1990.

Arctic Hares play. 21'' x 28''. (Private Collection)

St. Anthony's Harbor, Summer, 1990.

An iceberg, one of many that came into St. Anthony's Harbor in Newfoundland during the summer of 1990.

A newly made iceberg mat hooked for the Grenfell Handicrafts utilizes an old pattern. Diameter 17''. (Private Collection)

(Left) Two old mats from the days of the Grenfell Labrador Industries. (Courtesy of the Grenfell House Museum)

A polar bear sits comfortably upon his iceberg. 21'' x 29''.

The pattens for these new hooked mats were made by tracing old stencils. Polar bears remain a popular subject of the mats hooked for the Grenfell Handicrafts today.

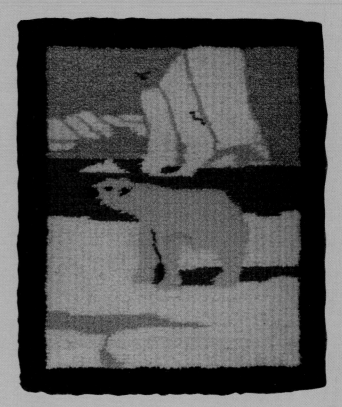

A polar bear upon his ice pan. 11'' x 13''. (Courtesy of Schiffer Publishing, Ltd.)

Iceberg and polar bear. 10'' x 11''. (Private Collection)

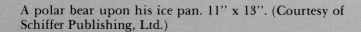

Ayer Antique designed by Pearl McGown and hooked by
Una Corriveau. 40'' x 85''. (Courtesy of Una Corriveau)
(Photo by Robert Moshimer)

Pearl McGown

Strolling through a New England antiques show during opening hours, you are likely to spot assorted hooked rugs of varying vintages. With luck, you might find animals, geometric designs, and recognizable Frost patterns all hooked during the second half of the 1800s. In harmony, among those of greater age, are finely hooked and artistically rendered floral rugs that date from the 1930s to the present. These hooked treasures are decorated with true to life floral sprays and elaborate twisting scrolls. The precisely detailed, delicate flowers hooked from shades of dyed wool material appear to be garden fresh. Roses are so exact in nature, you almost sense a hint of their light fragrance.

Rugs hooked during the 1930s and 40s were not merely floor coverings, but painstakingly planned and crafted still lifes in wool, many of which were never allowed to be walked upon. The availability of a hand operated cutting machine made it possible to slice wool fabric into 3/32'' wide strips. These spaghetti thin strips enabled workers to hook rugs of extremely fine texture and achieve accurate detail in the subjects they portrayed. The use of pre-stamped designs was frequent and though originality took a back seat, there was no denying that the finished products were rugs of great beauty and value.

Though these beautiful, flowered rugs fall short of the one hundred plus years required to qualify them as true antiques, their presence at antique shows is not discouraged, but rather encouraged by the insatiable demands of the collectors they attract. These underage new comers to the antique market are the product of rug hooking in the 1930s. Instrumental to the success of this spirited revival was Pearl K. McGown. Recognized as a designer of exquisite patterns, instructor of hooking teachers nation-wide, and author of four books on the craft, Pearl McGown gained notoriety as the "Grande Dame" of rug hooking.

Born in the small, rural town of Clinton, Massachusetts in 1892, Pearl was one of eleven children. Her father was a local building contractor and skilled draftsman. She spent her teenage years working in his office, while attending secretarial school at night. Exposure to the techniques of mechanical drawing fascinated the young woman and her acquired skill would prove to be an asset in the years that lay ahead.

Portrait of Pearl McGown holding her book *Color in Hooked Rugs.* (Photo courtesy of Meredith LeBeau)

A partially hooked Pearl McGown floral pattern with swatches of dyed wool, cut strips, and McGown Hook.

Married at the age of twenty-two, Pearl had one son, Winthrop. To make ends meet during a time when America was feeling the effects of the 1929 Wall Street Crash and the Depression, Pearl secured a position as a secretary in a law office near her West Boylston home. During this period, she became acquainted with Caroline Saunders, a talented rug hooking teacher. Aware of her drafting experience, Mrs. Saunders persuaded Pearl to design and print the burlap rug patterns needed by her many students. In spite of limited working space and simple tools, Pearl was able to produce patterns that pleased both teacher and pupils.

Requests for more and varied patterns sent Pearl searching antique shops for old hooked rugs, the source of inspiration for many of her designs. The earned income from this new venture provided capital for purchasing the larger amounts of burlap needed to keep up with the demands of incoming orders. With family members coming to her aid, Pearl not only filled the requests of Mrs. Saunder's students, but responded to inquiries from other rug hookers by starting a small mail order business. Hard working and driven to succeed, Pearl continued to work days as a legal secretary; laboring nights and into the early hours of the morning, she composed and stamped her rug patterns.

The revival of rug hooking was welcomed with much enthusiasm. In response to eager admirers longing for the treasures made from burlap and rag, Caroline Saunders, assisted by Pearl McGown, sponsored hooked rug exhibits, welcoming the inquisitive public. The gatherings served as a showcase for students, designers, and teachers and became a profitable promotion arena for manufacturers of hooked rug supplies. The exhibits proved to be successful in recruiting new hookers. Anxious students lined up, awaiting classes and qualified instructors.

Due to differing opinions concerning the instruction of future teachers and quarrels over ownership of rug designs, Pearl McGown and Caroline Saunders dissolved their working relationship. Mrs. Saunders continued to share her talents with a following of grateful students. Pearl worked toward earning a reputation that would make hers a household name in the homes of rug hookers across the United States.

Convinced that supplying the demand for qualified instructors was the key to rug hooking's vitality, Pearl established herself as a teacher of teachers. Her methods of instruction were strict and disciplined. Her apprentices were schooled in the art of dyeing and were carefully trained to hook lifelike flowers and fruits, among other things. Those who were chosen to study with Pearl were meticulously groomed to be teachers of the McGown Method. The rugs hooked by these talented ladies were exquisite. From East Coast to West Coast, the McGown teachers attracted dedicated pupils, sold Pearl's original design patterns, and continued the cycle of training new instructors.

The 1940s brought the outbreak of World War II and a plea from the American Red Cross for qualified crafts people. Patriotically, Pearl and twenty-seven of her teachers and their students volunteered at a local veteran's hospital. Four hundred wounded servicemen, under the direction of the McGown ladies, occupied their recuperating time, hooking rugs. Patterns were made by copying the insignia of the Army, Navy, and Air Corps. Foreseeing that the war time gas shortages and the embargo on imported burlap could bring the interest in rug hooking to a halt, Pearl composed a ten issue per year bulletin filled with hooking news and tips. This "Letter Service" inspired rug makers to continue their craft in spite of adverse conditions and maintained an open line of communication between hookers. The popularity of the bulletin outlasted the war.

As the interest in rug hooking rose to an all time high, the huge bolts of burlap and the equipment used by Pearl overwhelmed her shrinking living quarters. The dream of expansion came true in 1945 when Pearl purchased a larger home, known as Rose Cottage. Relying on her secretarial job for funds

Memoria designed by Pearl McGown and hooked by Jane Curtin. The rug was started in 1960, and put away when discouraged by her teacher's comment that the daffodils resembled goldfish. In 1982, the rug was unpacked and completed. Hooked on one end, the dates it was begun and finished and rug maker's name. The names of her two granddaughters are hooked on the opposite end. 40'' x 78''. (Courtesy of Jane Curtin)

Memoria designed by Pearl McGown and recently hooked by Cheryl Orcutt. 40'' x 80''. (Courtesy of the Art Underfoot™ Treasury Collection)

A burlap pattern depicting Rose Cottage, which Pearl gave to teachers and friends during the holiday season. 12" x 16".

The living room of Rose Cottage. Pictured are *Victorian Square*, *Tradition*, and *Chilcott Scroll*. (Information Courtesy of Jane McGown Flynn)

The dining room of Rose Cottage. Underneath the table is *Maltese Cross*. (Information Courtesy of Jane McGown Flynn)

The Studio at Rose Cottage. Above the fireplace hangs *The Prize Rug,* on the floor one corner of *New England Twist, Prize Octagon,* and *Lincoln Log Cabin.* Over the radiator, *Roseada* is displayed. (Information Courtesy of Jane McGown Flynn)

Roseada designed by Pearl McGown. Circa 1940. 48'' x 78''. (Collection of D.C. Wolff)

Roseada designed by Pearl McGown. Marked 46 (1946). 48'' x 78''. (Private Collection of S. Segal)

and putting her drafting skills to use, Rose Cottage was remodeled to provide a storage area for materials and tools, to house a large classroom, and to give adequate floor and wall space to showcase finished rugs. Though Rose Cottage was Pearl's private residence, the public was welcome to drop in any afternoon, Monday through Friday. Visitors from across the United States, Canada, and several foreign countries stood patiently in line waiting to view the interior of Rose Cottage, mecca for rug hookers and home of the famous Pearl McGown.

Family members were instrumental to the success of her business, and along with other workers, Pearl employed three of her six sisters. May, living with Pearl in earlier days, served as her assistant. Sylvia, retired from a banking career, acted as bookkeeper. Kaddy, as Pearl's agent, traveled in 1946 to California, where in the Sherman Oaks district she opened a rug

A hand cranked cutter made easy work of slicing wool fabric into thin uniform strips.

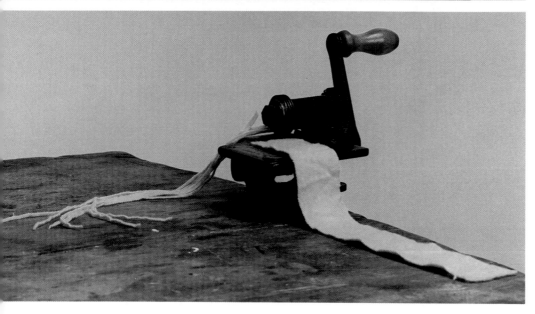

Opposite page:
Catherine Duignan works on *Alliance*, a design by Pearl McGown. (Photo Courtesy of Bob Kurtz)

134

hooking shop and offered classes. A frequent passerby, named Clark Gable, would often pause and admire the fine rugs on display. By 1948 Pearl's business was incorporated and the following year, a financially secure Pearl retired from her position as legal secretary, a job she had held for twenty-five years.

Of vital importance to Pearl McGown, her teachers, and their students were the annual hooked rug exhibits. From the beginning of 1940 and throughout most of the 50s, the carefully planned events attracted rug hookers nationwide. Each May, over three hundred and fifty rugs and hundreds of small hooked pieces were sent from nearly every state and assembled and displayed for audiences that swelled to over 5,000. These eagerly anticipated shows continued until 1957, when exhaustion took its toll upon Pearl and the many workers who were required to set up the enormous halls. In addition to hooked rug exhibits, there were scores of McGown teacher conferences and workshops, hooking bees, week long seminars, and overnight McGown rug hooking camps. The Northern rug hookers met in harmony with the Southern rug hookers to exchange ideas and develop lifelong friendships. Attending as many of these meetings as possible, was Pearl McGown.

White Flower Sampler designed by Pearl McGown. 14'' x 18''. (Private Collection of Susan Goldberg) (Photo by Joan Moshimer)

A teacher's sampler of a country church designed by Pearl McGown. A gift to the author from dear friend and fellow rug hooker, Dot Abbott. Hooked in the 1980s by Dot. 13'' x 17''.

Unicorn in Captivity designed by Pearl McGown, inspired by an early tapestry of the same name in The Cloisters. (Metropolitan Museum of Art), and hooked by Margaret Amdur. 24'' x 36''. (Courtesy of Margaret Amdur) (Photo by Bob Kurtz)

Chair seat/pillow top designed by Pearl McGown and recently hooked by Marie Dessureau. Diameter 14''. (Courtesy of the Art Underfoot™ Treasury Collection)

A handbag made from a Pearl McGown design. Hooked by Margaret Amdur. (Courtesy of Margaret Amdur) (Photo by Bob Kurtz)

Iris pillow designed by Pearl McGown and newly hooked by Marie Dessureau. 14'' x 14''. (Courtesy of the Art Underfoot™ Treasury Collection)

Tulips and Lilacs designed by Pearl McGown. 17'' x 15''. (Private Collection of Susan Goldberg) (Photo by Joan Moshimer)

Rose Tile designed by Pearl McGown and hooked by Dot Abbott in the 1980s. 7'' x 7''.

137

Chilcott Runner designed by Pearl McGown. Circa 1940.
27" x 70". (Private Collection)

Plume Poppy designed by Pearl McGown and recently
hooked by Betty McClentic. 37" x 29". (Courtesy of the Art
Underfoot™ Treasury Collection)

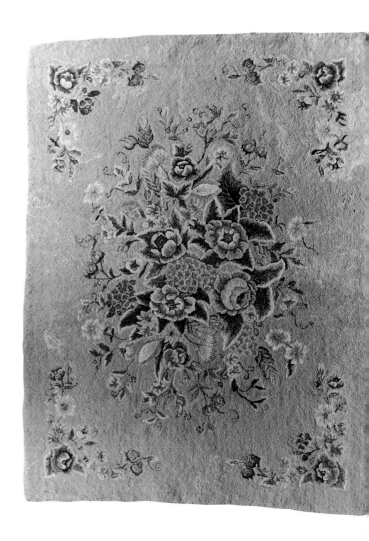

Miller Floral designed by Pearl McGown and hooked by
Patricia DeForest in the 1940s. 50" x 67". (Courtesy of
Patricia DeForest) (Photo by Bob Kurtz)

Rug hookers and their instructor meet every two weeks to work and exchange ideas. The group has been together for over ten years and plans to continue for many more. (Photo by Bob Kurtz)

Maltese Cross designed by Pearl McGown. 1940-1960. 37'' x 55''.

Leaves No. 226 designed by Pearl McGown. Circa 1940. 27'' x 72''.

Alice in Wonderland designed by Pearl McGown and hooked by Olive Sauer, 31″ x 60″. (Courtesy of Olive Sauer) (Photo by Bob Kurtz)

The Grand Bouquet designed by Jane McGown Flynn and newly hooked by Ruth Roccia. 24″ x 36″. (Courtesy of the Art Underfoot™ Treasury Collection)

Bottles designed by Pearl McGown. 14″ x 17″. (Private Collection of Susan Goldberg) (Photo by Joan Moshimer)

Leaving the established business in the capable hands of her staff and family, Pearl was able to travel more often. Foreign sights inspired new hooked rug designs. Geometric, Oriental, and crewel patterns, as well as others, were added to the McGown collection. Though more and more designers flooded the pattern market, Pearl maintained her quota of releasing a dozen new patterns per month and an additional two dozen or more small pieces.

As the years passed, advancing age and health problems caused Pearl to reluctantly assign to others the duties she had once handled. Family, teachers, and staff undertook the additional tasks, while granddaughter, Jane, a talented designer and hooked rug enthusiast, continued to write the bulletin, "Letter Service".

In 1970, the rights to the McGown designs, all aspects of the business, and many of the rugs displayed at Rose Cottage were sold to Old Sturbridge Village of Sturbridge, Massachusetts, an organization noted for its historical preservation projects. Shortly after the business changed hands, Rose Cottage was sold and Pearl moved into an apartment of more manageable size. She continued to correspond with the many teachers and friends she had gathered during her forty years of rug hooking. When health permitted, she attended conferences of McGown teachers.

In January, 1983, Pearl McGown quietly passed away, leaving behind a legacy. During her many years of service to the rug hooking community, Pearl McGown trained noteworthy and talented teachers. Many remained faithful admirers of the rigid McGown Method. Others abandoned her rules and pursued their own creativity, shedding yet another light upon the rug hooking world. Listed in the *Who's Who of American Women* of 1975-1976, author of four books and numerous pamphlets still in use, Pearl McGown inspired all involved with hooked rugs. Today her methods continue to be taught and her designs reprinted for the many rug hookers who remain loyal McGown followers.

Jane McGown Flynn inherited her grandmother's love for rug hooking and talent for designing patterns. A skilled teacher, artist, and promoter of the craft, Jane has contributed greatly to the growth and development of rug hooking today.

Geometric Floral designed by Jane McGown Flynn and hooked in 1990 by Lillian Nutting. 26" x 42". (Courtesy of the Art Underfoot™ Treasury Collection)

141

Aurora Rose. Designed and hooked by Joan Moshimer.
Diameter 44''. (Photo by Robert Moshimer)

Joan Moshimer

To the good fortune of all, the craft of rug hooking has not fallen victim to the computerized, fast paced world that we live in today. Houses equipped with central heat and machine made carpeting have relinquished us from the need to create our own floor coverings for warmth. For the majority of adults with hectic work schedules, there is little time for afternoon teas and rug hooking bees. Yet, in spite of all modern conveniences and the lack of leisure hours, women and men continue to hook rugs, just as they did in the second half of the 1800s.

In order for hooking to continue its vitality from one generation to the next, there must be a source of inspiration and encouragement to keep the craft alive and developing. The preceding chapters of this book are dedicated to those who loved and promoted the craft in days gone by. Rug hooking is alive and well in the 1990s. A New Zealand born artist, brought to the United States by her husband after World War II, was largely responsible during the 1970s and faithfully thereafter, for renewing an interest in rug hooking.

Joan Leith Moshimer was born and educated in Auckland. She attended the Elam School of Art and pursued a commercial art career. World War II brought Warrant Officer Robert Moshimer to New Zealand for a much deserved rest following his brave efforts to safely evacuate 5,000 G.I.'s from a sinking ship. Bob and Joan met, fell in love, and married in Auckland. At war's end, Bob brought the new Mrs. Moshimer half way around the world to his home in Portland, Maine where they purchased a large Victorian vintage house. On a budget that could not afford Oriental carpets, and living in a house full of bare wooden floors, Joan was inspired to seek the craft of rug hooking. Initially self-taught with the aid of limited information, Joan sought out local rug hooking teachers and studied with them. The retirement of her own instructor and the foresight to urge Joan to teach helped to shape a hobby into a full time career. Rug hooking classes under Joan's direction proved enjoyable to both teacher and the growing enrollment of students. Though monetary rewards were limited at $2.50 for two days of instruction per week, Joan's earnings, saved for over four years, enabled her to publish a rug pattern catalog of her own designs.

While Bob managed a local glass company and helped Joan to raise their young son and daughter, they spent their evenings in the attic office working on enlarging their small but growing company. The company was dedicated to supplying the needs of all rug hookers and would soon become a full time venture. After

Joan Moshimer stands in front of *Cumberland Crewel*, a rug she designed and hooked. 8' x 10'. (Photo by Robert Moshimer)

Strawberry Basket. Designed by Joan Moshimer and hooked by Michael Santos. Many men enjoy rug hooking and this was Michael's first attempt. The background color is the result of dyeing white wool with yellow onion skins. 25'' x 42''. (Courtesy of Michael Santos)

Jolly Olde St. Nick. Designed and hooked by Joan Moshimer. 27'' x 44''. (Photo by Robert Moshimer)

Young Stilt. Hooked on dyed wool. Designed and hooked by Joan Moshimer. 11'' x 18''. (Photo by Robert Moshimer)

Pheasant. Designed and hooked by Joan Moshimer. 15'' x 21''. (Photo by Robert Moshimer)

Heartfelt Cats designed and hooked by Joan Moshimer 29'' x 40''. (Photo by Robert Moshimer)

Teddy Bear Story Time. Designed and hooked by Joan Moshimer. 29'' x 41''. (Photo by Robert Moshimer)

Joanne's Quilt. A quilt made by Joanne Neville inspired this design. Designed and hooked by Joan Moshimer. 26" x 41". (Photo by Robert Moshimer)

purchasing the century old W. Cushing Company, rug hookers and braiders were assured that the fine line of dyes and hooking supplies would continue.

By virtue of her superior hooking and teaching skills, Joan was chosen to study with the revered Pearl McGown, master instructor of hooking teachers and designer of exquisite floral patterns. Joan remained a loyal McGown teacher for several years, but ultimately felt that rug hooking should reflect more individual creativity than the McGown Method allowed. The introduction, or rather the actual return to a less structured and more creative rug hooking appealed to many novice rug hookers. During 1968, an eager audience followed the Moshimers from their Portland attic office to the opening of Joan's studio in Kennebunkport, Maine.

Kennebunkport, Maine is known to most as the summer home of the President and First Lady, George and Barbara Bush. The scenic crashing waves of Walker's Point are the location of many presidential conferences, international meetings, and news briefs of world importance. But to thousands of rug hookers across the United States, Canada, and as far north as the Labrador shores, Kennebunkport is the home of the W. Cushing and Company, suppliers of everything a rug hooker could ever need. More importantly, the coastline community is the home of Joan Moshimer. The publishing of Joan's book, *The Complete Rug Hooker* during the 1970s inspired many to try the craft and lead to yet another revival of interest. Under the roof of her studio, she wrote and edited *Rug Hooker News and Views*, a popular magazine which attracted an international audience. The rights to the eighteen year old publication were sold in 1989 to Stackpole Publishers who now distribute *Rug Hooking*, a successful continuation of Joan's initial efforts. As the business grew, Bob retired from his own career and devoted his efforts to the rug hooking business, accompanying Joan on her many lectures, demonstrations, and fact finding jaunts. Their son Paul is the company's manager and his wife Pat, is in charge of printing patterns. Because of a fine reputation and an undeniable devotion to the craft, their business, W. Cushing and Company, has been chosen to carry on the lines of many famous hooked rug pattern designers of the past.

The author has a special fondness for both Joan and Bob Moshimer. Many years ago, I was invited to be interviewed for a spot in *Rug Hooker News and Views*. Eager to show my collection of old "ratty rugs" to someone who might understand my determination to give life back to doomed hooked rugs of disrepair, I was welcomed by a genuinely warm and gracious lady who was indeed interested in my work and who heartily encouraged my efforts. Surrounded in her studio by hooked treasures of all styles and dimensions, what impressed me most was how freely Joan gave of her time and great knowledge. During a long association and friendship, her giving nature and devotion to the craft of rug hooking, a trait possessed by both Joan and Bob Moshimer, has never ceased. It would be improper and incorrect to assume that Joan Moshimer single-handedly revived the interest in rug hooking. Many, many talented teachers, designers, and rug hooking artists have contributed greatly to the growth and development of the craft. If modern day rug hookers were asked to appoint a leader, however, Joan Moshimer would be first in line.

Sandringham. Designed by Joan Moshimer and hooked by Jane Curtin. 24'' x 34''. (Courtesy of Jane Curtin)

Idol. Designed by Joan Moshimer and hooked by Jane Curtin. 25'' x 38''. (Courtesy of Jane Curtin)

147

The Newfoundland coastline—August 1990.

Familiar surroundings serve as a source of inspiration for
many mat and rug hookers.

A Rug of Your Own

Rug hooking is a simple and easy craft to learn. With some practice, the hook will feel comfortable in your hand and you will be able to pull loops through the burlap's weave with lightening speed. The how-to steps shown introduce you to the technique of hooking. Once the basic skill is mastered, the door to your own creativity is wide open.

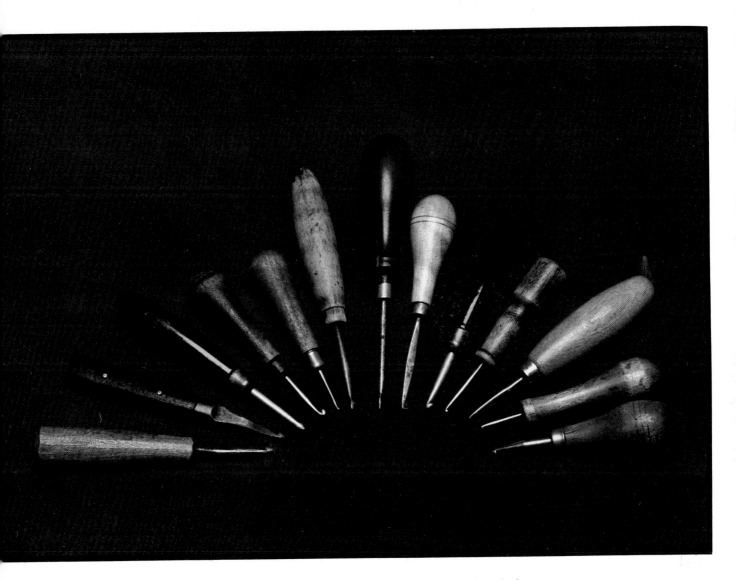

An assortment of hooks, both old and new, hand crafted and machine manufactured.

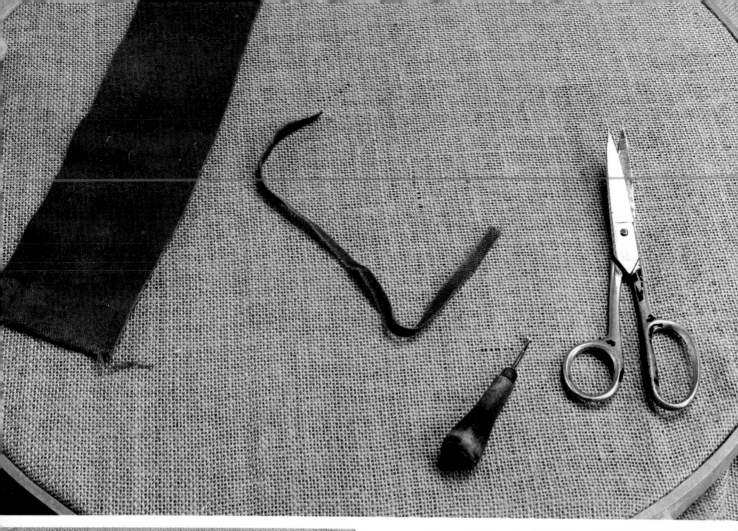

Materials required for hooking a rug: fabric (wool material is recommended) cut into strips, burlap for a foundation, hook and scissors. The burlap can be held taut by tacking or sewing to a frame or using hooking hoops.

Strips can easily be cut by hand. A length of about 10'' is best; the width can vary from ⅛'' to ½''.

Though there is no right or wrong way, I suggest holding your hook as you would a pencil. The hand which holds the hook is placed on the top surface of the burlap. Beneath the burlap, the thumb and fore finger of your other hand holds the cut strip and will guide the strip into the crook of your hook.

Poke the hook through an opening in the weave of the burlap. Grab the strip with your hook.

Pull the end of the strip up through the weave to the top of the burlap.

Close to the end you just pulled up, poke the hook down through an opening in the weave of the burlap and pull more of the strip up to the top surface.

Pull the loop up about ½''.

Repeat the process. Place your hook near the loop that was just pulled up, poke through the burlap and draw up another loop. Make sure the guide hand beneath the burlap keeps the strip straight, not letting it twist or bunch up.

With practice your loops will become evenly spaced and of equal height.

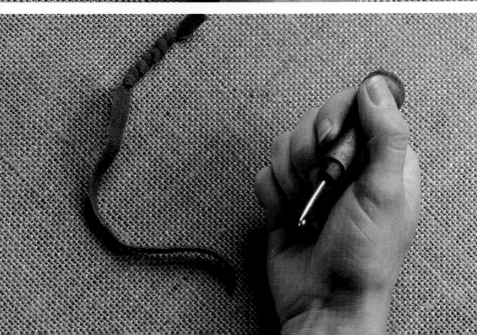

When ending your row of hooking, pull the remainder of the strip to the top surface.

Cut the two ends off so they are of the same height as your loops. All beginnings and ends of strips are pulled to the surface and clipped. The underside of the burlap should be neat, with no strips hanging. As you continue to hook, pack your loops closely together. Before you know it, you have hooked a good size area.

Hooking using two different width strips. The bottom row shows the tops of all loops have been clipped. This step is often used when hooking Oriental patterns.

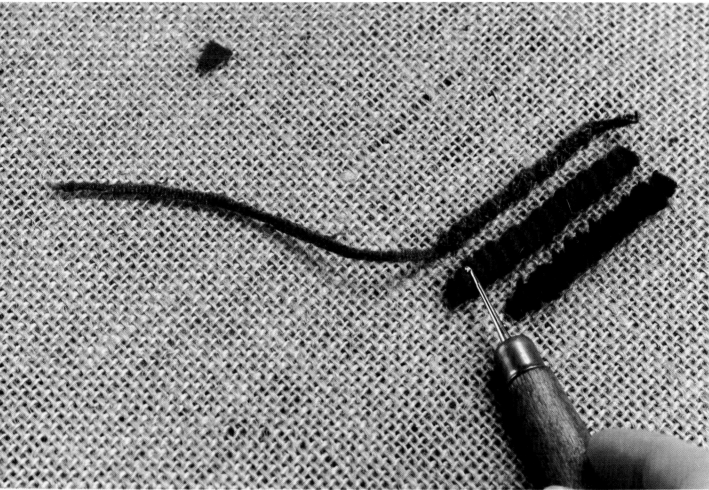

Preservation for the Future

Hooked rugs are sensitive textiles; they require and deserve special care. The proper treatment of hand crafted rugs will result in increased longevity and monetary value.

Light cleaning of a hooked rug can be accomplished by gently sweeping the front and back surfaces with a broom or soft bristle brush. Refrain from shaking or beating. The sharp, jerking motions will break the threads of the rug's burlap or linen foundation and cause holes to develop. DO NOT USE A VACUUM CLEANER ON ANY HOOKED RUG. Powerful suction, combined with rotating brushes will weaken and sever the burlap's weave. Vacuum cleaners can suck up entire sections of hooking, leaving you with a rug that resembles a slice of Swiss cheese.

Should more thorough attention be warranted, hooked rugs can be cleansed with a mild soap and water mixture or commercial shampoo made expressly for hooked rugs. Begin by removing all surface dirt with a broom or brush. Mix together a solution of cold water and enough soap to made suds. The suds, not the liquid will do the cleaning. Check that no colors in the rug will run or bleed by daubing the underside with some suds. Allow the test areas to dry. If all fabrics are colorfast, proceed with cleaning the front surface. With a soft brush or white cotton cloth, gently scrub in small circular motions, using the suds and as little of the water as possible. When the process is completed, blot up any excess moisture with a white towel. Lay the rug flat until completely dry. Do not hang a damp hooked rug on a rod or clothesline. If needed, repeat the cleaning procedure on heavily stained areas. Hooked rugs should never be submerged in water or hosed down. The threads of the burlap base tend to rot from the soaking.

Never, under any circumstances clean a hooked rug in a washing machine-the results are disastrous. Due to their somewhat delicate nature, all hooked rugs should be cleaned by hand. The burlap and rag textiles quickly deteriorate when subjected to strong chemicals and harsh treatment.

The range of prices for hooked rugs is wide and varied. Pristine antique rugs have sold for tens of thousands of dollars, while examples of fine hooked handiwork have been had for a mere twenty dollars. When purchasing a hooked rug, condition is important. Avoid buying rugs whose underside is covered with a latex or rubber backing. Originally sold in the 1940s and 1950s as a preservative for crafts, the painted-on coating dries, cracks and can not be successfully removed without damaging the rug, making repairs virtually impossible. If a hooked rug is so dry and brittle that a powder forms when the foundation is squeezed, it should be passed. The rug's fragile condition makes it not fit for floor use and an unlikely candidate for restoration. Hooked rugs with small patches and well executed repairs are worth purchasing. As a functioning part of the household, few rugs survived without some mending.

Many hooked rugs, still useful and decorative, but in need of repair can be bought for reasonable prices. If you are unable to undertake a repair project yourself, seek out the services of a professional hooked rug restorer. Repair work demands patience, an eye for detail and color, hand sewing and hooking skills. Hasty attempts to fix a rug with iron-on patches, glue, tape or latex will drastically reduce the value of the rug and add to the expense of having a professional restorer undo (if possible) your mistakes.

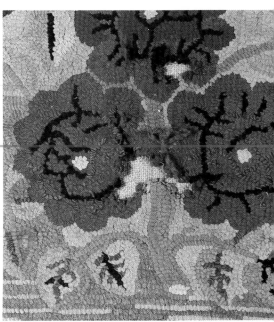

Fixing your own rugs can save money and bring personal satisfaction in knowing you rescued a "doomed" textile. To repair a small hole, sew a burlap patch beneath the affected area. Using strong carpet thread, stitch all broken ends of old burlap and loose hooked loops to the patch. Once your sewing is completed and the edges of the hole are secure to the patch, hook in the missing portion. Pay close attention to matching the original fabrics, colors, tightness, height of hooking, etc. Any worn edges of a hooked rug should be repaired and covered with a cotton twill binding, dyed to match a subdued color of the rug and sewn in place by hand. Rows of braiding stitched around the edges of a rug act as buffers against wear and fraying.

Hooked rugs can function as floor coverings or be displayed upon walls as textile art. Rugs that are large, cumbersome and heavy to lift should not be hung. The suspended weight will weaken and split the foundation, damaging the rug. Hooked pieces that are small and light in weight can be successfully displayed on walls without doing harm to the hand crafted work. By sewing a fabric sleeve on the back and inserting a wooden dowel or rod, a hooked rug can be hung as you would a painting. If corners of the rug curl or sides bow, the use of common or dress maker's pins to flatten the problems will neither damage the rug or the wall upon which it rests. Do not use nails, staples or any type of tape to support the textile.

When storing a hooked rug make sure it is clean and free from any moisture. Never fold a hooked rug. Always roll, with the right side out. By rolling with the front surface exposed, no strain is placed on the burlap base and it is less likely to weaken and split. Wrap the rolled rug in a white cloth (bed sheets are perfect); to discourage moths add some cedar chips or moth flakes and store where the temperature is dry and even. Extreme heat, prolonged sunlight and dampness can harm a hooked rug at rest. Do not place your stored rugs in plastic. Without circulating air, mildew can form and quickly rot your rug.

A piece of hooked rug was used to pad this antique stool.

Bibliography

Books

Batchelder, Martha. *The Art of Hooked Rug Making*. Peoria, Illinois: The Manual Arts Press, 1947.

Beatty, Alice and Mary Sargent. *The Hook Book*. Harrisburg, Pennsylvania: Stackpole Books, 1975.

Blanford, William B. and Elizabeth Blanford. *Beauport Impressions*. Boston: The Society for the Preservation of New England Antiquities, 1965.

Bowles, Ella Shannon. *Handmade Rugs*. New York: Garden City Publishing Co., Inc., 1937.

Frost, Edward Sands. *Hooked Rug Patterns*. Dearborn, Michigan: Greenfield Village and Henry Ford Museum, 1970.

Ketchum, William C. Jr. *Hooked Rugs*. New York: Harcourt, Brace, Jovanovich, 1976.

Kent, William Winthrop. *The Hooked Rug*. New York: Tudor Publishing Co., 1930.

Kent, William Winthrop. *Hooked Rug Design*. Springfield, Massachusetts: The Pond-Ekberg Company, 1949.

Kent, William Winthrop. *Rare Hooked Rugs*. Springfield, Massachusetts: The Pond-Ekberg Company, 1941.

Kopp, Joel and Kate. *American Hooked and Sewn Rugs*. New York: E. P. Dutton Inc., 1975.

McGown, Pearl K. *Color in Hooked Rugs*. Boston: Buck Printing Co., 1954.

McGown, Pearl K. *Dreams Beneath the Design*. Boston: Bruce Humphries Inc., 1939.

McGown, Pearl K. *The Lore and Lure of Hooked Rugs*. Acton, Massachusetts: Acton Press, 1966.

McGown, Pearl K. *You. . .Can Hook Rugs*. Boston: Buck Printing, 1951.

Moshimer, Joan. *The Complete Rug Hooker*. Boston: New York Graphic Society, 1975.

Phillips, Anna M. Laise. *Hooked Rugs and How to Make Them*. New York: The MacMillan Co., 1925.

Rex, Stella Hay. *Practical Hooked Rugs*. Asheville, Maine: Cobblesmith, 1975.

Ries, Estelle H. *American Rugs*. Cleveland, Ohio: The World Publishing Co., 1950.

Ryan, Nanette and Doreen Wright. *Garretts and Bluenose Rugs of Nova Scotia*. Halifax, 1990.

Safford, Carleton, L. and Robert Bishop. *America's Quilts and Coverlets*. New York: Weathervane Books, 1974.

Stratton, Charlotte Kimball. *Rug Hooking Made Easy*. New York: Harper and Brothers Publishers, 1955.

Taylor, Mary Perkins. *How To Make Hooked Rugs*. Philadelphia: David McKay Publishers, 1930.

Underhill, Vera Bisbee with Arthur J. Burks. *Creating Hooked Rugs*. New York: Coward-McCann, 1951.

Von Rosenstiel, Helene. *American Rugs and Carpets*. New York: William Morrow and Co., Inc., 1978.

Waugh, Elizabeth and Edith Foley. *Collecting Hooked Rugs*. New York: The Century Co., 1927.

Weissman, Judith Reiter and Wendy Lavitt. *Labors of Love*. New York: Alfred A. Knopf, 1987.

Articles

Dodge, Irene. "Philena Moxley's Embroidery Stamps." *Antiques* (August 1972): 251-253.

Hornidge, Marilis. "The Waldoboro Rug: A Tradition Lives." *The Weekly* (October 4, 1979): 21.

Libby, Steve. "Family Upholds Crafting Tradition." *Lewiston Journal* (December 4, 1982).

Luther, Jessie. "Hooked Mats." *Among Deep-Sea Fishers* (July 1916).

Moshimer, Joan. "Rugs of the Grenfell Mission." *Rug Hooker-News and Views* (July/August 1982): 140-141, 158.

Moshimer, Joan. "The Story of Philena Moxley and Her Printing Blocks." *Rug Hooker-News and Views* (July/August 1980): 133-134.

National Guild of Pearl K. McGown Rug Hookrafters Inc., *Newsletter*, Vol. 12. No. 1. (March 1983): 1-56.

Pennington, Sam. "The Waldoboro Rug." *The Weekly* (August 10, 1979): 14.

Spring, Annie. "Legacy from the House of Burnham." *Rug Hooking*, Vol. II. No. 5. (January/February 1991): 2-7.

Spring, Annie. "The House of Burnham." *Rug Hooker-News and Views* (January/February 1983): 60-66.

Thomas, Gordon W. "The International Grenfell Association-Its Role in Northern Newfoundland and Labrador. Part I: The Early Days." *CMA Journal*, Vol, 118. (February 4, 1978): 308-310.

The Waldoborough Historical Society. "Waldoboro's History-A brief History of a Beautiful Downeast Town on Maine's Mid-Coast." (June 1971).

Frost pattern No. 59. Touches of yellow and gold enhance this floral hooked rug. Circa 1890. 20" x 39". (Private Collection)

Index